A Christian Guide to Prosperous Living

Joseph E. Hein

National Library of Canada Cataloguing in Publication

Hein, Joseph E., 1972-
A Christian guide to prosperous living / Joseph E. Hein.

Includes bibliographical references.
ISBN 1-4120-0541-8

I. Title.

BV4598.3.H44 2003 248.4 C2003-903829-7

TRAFFORD

This book was published *on-demand* in cooperation with Trafford Publishing. On-demand publishing is a unique process and service of making a book available for retail sale to the public taking advantage of on-demand manufacturing and Internet marketing. **On-demand publishing** includes promotions, retail sales, manufacturing, order fulfilment, accounting and collecting royalties on behalf of the author.

Suite 6E, 2333 Government St., Victoria, B.C. V8T 4P4, CANADA
Phone 250-383-6864 Toll-free 1-888-232-4444 (Canada & US)
Fax 250-383-6804 E-mail sales@trafford.com
Web site www.trafford.com TRAFFORD PUBLISHING IS A DIVISION OF TRAFFORD HOLDINGS LTD.
Trafford Catalogue #03-0910 www.trafford.com/robots/03-0910.html

10 9 8 7 6 5 4 3 2

This book is dedicated with extra love, to my exceptional wife, Linda, my incredible son, Braden, and my wonderful Parents-in-Law, Marvin and NanJean Kiesow.

Special thanks to my Sister, Rella, who through all things, good, bad, and even ugly, was there with encouragement and support.

Thanks to my Grandfather Alvin Hein for all that you have given me in my life, including attention, time, advice, love, and most of all, hope, of who I am, and who I am to become.

Thanks to my Parents, Janet and Jim, for all of the memories that I have of my childhood. Each day, although not always peachy, was filled with promise and hope. Thank you for your support!

Thanks to my Friends in class #54 and my Professors at Silver Lake College in Manitowoc, my Friends and Educators at Oakfield High School, and my Friends and Educators at U.W. Center Fond du Lac.

In loving memory of Grandma Linda Hein, Grandma Loretta Bouzek, Grandpa John Rawlins, and my Aunt Betty . These positively dynamic and loving individuals had tremendous influence on all of my thoughts and beliefs.

Table of Contents

The Life Force Inside You

I know how it is, you're going through life and you know just exactly what it is you want, but you have no idea how to get it. Or, things begin to go wrong for you at the most inopportune time. Challenges arise on a daily basis causing a major struggle in your mindset about which way to go with your decisions, or the decisions that you make seem to not take on the shape of resolution or success that you had hoped for.

These challenges and many others, face all people in all walks of life on a daily basis, but there is a way to overcome them. A simple, strategic way that calls on your ability to relate and co-exist with God, the Creator of all things, and the blessings that he keeps flowing inside you. The blessings are a divine energy that you can tap into on a daily basis, or leave flowing for others to use from you. It is the energy that allows you to live a life that is free from worry or doubt, free from pain and frustration, free from the rigors of an uncertain life that the rest of the world has to face. It is an energy that allows you to make the life that you want for yourself.

Throughout the pages of this book I will teach you how this is all possible in easy to understand plain talk. I will guide you through the steps that your body and mind take in the process of decision making, healing, forgiving others, gaining success and prosperity, and achieving all of your personal dreams and goals. You will in the process, relieve yourself of negative thoughts, negative feelings, and negative energies, on your ultimate quest to become everything you want to become.

This book was written with you in mind. Helping you to fulfill the great accomplishments you were born to achieve is its only purpose. Nobody can claim, if they fail to accomplish their dreams, that it was not meant to be. Nor can anyone claim that they were not capable of accomplishing their dreams, because we all have the tools necessary to accomplish everything we need and desire, built right inside of us. The challenge then lies in figuring out how to use our talents to accomplish the things we want. In the next few chapters I will show you step by step how to systematically go about making your dreams happen.

Day after day We read about how somebody did something great, became a hero, invented the next great gadget, or pioneered a successful up-and-coming company. But, we don't realize that we all have the ability to do those very same things. There are thousands of ways that people could think of to become successful, everybody's ideas different than another. You could achieve financial independence, and become free of the fear that sometimes seems to have a stranglehold on your life. Whether it's developing a new invention that gets you there, changing your career path, or just changing your mind, there are thousands of ways for you to get where you want to be and achieve the things you want.

I say, and have always said that we are programmed and destined for success to achieve all our life's ambitions. There is one thing you must do and do very well however, and that is to have your thoughts and your desires outlined and organized. You have to extinguish all of your negative thoughts, and think about what will come when you start to put your dreams and goals in the forefront of your life. This is not that difficult and I will show you step-by-step foolproof actions that you can take today and everyday to get you where you want to be.

How do I identify my goals and dreams, and just what is achievable? This is the biggest challenge to those that don't know how to achieve their goals and dreams. The lack of focus and commitment has held you back. But the key to achieving these dreams is not a secret, if you are an organized person with clearly defined goals who can follow instructions, you will achieve your goals and dreams. If you are not an organized person with clearly defined goals, but can still follow instructions, this is your lucky day. What you have here in front of you is the guide to achieving all of your goals and dreams in a short book. I will cover everything with you from front to back. Stored up inside of you are vast amounts of wealth that after you turn on your endless fountain of love and intelligence, will come flowing from you, enriching your life and the lives of everyone around you.

Utilizing Your Treasures and Talents

You will find that all successful people in life attribute their success not to luck such as being in the right place at the right time, but to the control of the things they can control and the acceptance of things they can not. Successful people rightfully attribute their successes to the law of life. Cause and effect is the ruler of their lives and the foundation of their belief; it is the one law that rules their world. They rightfully believe that whatever they desire and believe to be true, will come true. These people know that whatever they impress upon their subconscious mind will be expressed in the experiences of their life. The way you really think and feel in your heart and mind helps you to rule over every phase of your life.

Believe in the things that will bring about good and beneficial results and lead you to gifts and blessings. Think about those things that will enrich your life and give you prosperity. Dwell on those things that give you pleasure and peace, and become fully absorbed in those things that give you joy and enrichment. Do not ever resign yourself to say that "it is not my day" or "perhaps I will have better luck next time." To say these things leaves you to base all of life's occurrences on chance and not onto the great mental, physical, and spiritual tools you have employed to achieve them.

You can however believe in good fortune, because good fortune is given to you by the Great

Power above; it is not the same as chance or luck. A person who believes that luck directs his future is waiting for success, happiness, and riches to come his way. He believes that things will go his way without work and thought being paid to it. This person paces or lies around, or does things that do not necessarily keep him on track toward his life's ambition, and expects a prize to show up at his doorstep. This is the man who expects to win the lottery with or without buying a ticket.

A person who sculpts and shapes his future with his attitude and the power of his mind, knows that he was born to succeed and was given all the tools for success at his birth. He knows that as he goes about doing the work that will shape his future, he is forging an exceptional life for himself. His life is filled with success and notable milestones along the way, where he has measured and can continue to measure the great successes of his life. As this person looks back at the milestones with great pride and accomplishment, he can continue in his progress knowing that what has gotten him to that point is what will guide him sailing ever so steadily into the future with fondness and appreciation for what he has.

Indeed, good fortune will abound for the industrious person, because he is at work in his mind everyday making room for more good fortune. This person is paving the way and making more room for the greater fortunes, that through arduous work, will come to him. Don't let your mind rest on your accomplishments, but challenge it everyday to devise a just way to continue to accomplish those things which you want in your life. The mind, spirit, and body are not happy if you settle for your lot in life, because they were designed altogether as a smooth functioning machine to set goals and desires and achieve them.

You Reap What You Sow

The mind is a vast and complex organ fortified with energy. It is in this place that we often fail to look to find answers to the problems and issues that face us on a regular basis. Most of us believe that the only action that takes place is that action that is seen and measured upon the external world. The truth is, a profound reaction takes place in your life when you set your thoughts onto the good and the vibrant things in life, seen or unseen. When you fixate and dwell on the good things that you have in mind for your life and the lives of others, it is as if you have done something very tangible to uplift and motivate yourself and them. When you think in a benevolent and confident fashion, good fortune and lasting benefits will follow.

In order to experience good fortune you have to put your talents to good use. The talents, are your gifts such as the power of your mind, your good spirit, your money, and your well wishes. Realizing that it is the thoughts, emotions, and reactions to life that shape the rest of your life and assist in the shaping of the lives around you, brings a very tangible and appreciative quality to your talents. You reap what you sow. Good Thoughts will bring about good experiences and bad thoughts will bring about bad experiences in your life.

Positive and industrious thoughts will create in you a person who does not let grass grow under his feet.

It is never twisted fate that leaves a man in desperation, rather it is the life lived in corrupt, cancerous, and wicked thinking which some people nurture and breed in their minds. When these corrupt thoughts reach a point of overfill in the mind, they are brought about into this world in the course of a person's actions. It is inexcusable to think poor and devious thoughts. It is these devious thoughts that lead people to desperation and suffering. You can not think self-defeating and self-deprecating thoughts, because these will lead you down a path where you will feel great sadness and isolation from the good things of the world.

I have met many people in my time that do a lot of great things for people. They seem to enjoy doing people favors and helping them out, but deep down inside they have confided, they don't feel like they care much about others. They say that they are only doing it to get by or get ahead in the world. They are really not performing a service to others because they don't have a true desire to help people. This is the kind of behavior that is noticeably helpful, but the thoughts that belie their actions show the shallowness and insincerity of the person. Great gifts, great fortune, and great talents will never be in the possession of people who only serve in order to make a favorable impression on other people.

Great gifts will also not accompany the people who don't have faith that great gifts will come their way. It is essential to think well and keep your thoughts pure. Belief in good produces good, no matter what demeanor is visible to the outside world. This is why good things sometimes happen to seemingly bad people and bad things sometimes happen to seemingly good people. If your thoughts are pure and your actions are good, then good consequences will always follow you.

Aim For The Stars, You May Hit The Moon

The power of your dreams is a preview to the thoughts that you think. As you want to always think good thoughts, you also want to have lofty dreams. These dreams will have you thinking of good all the time. Your thoughts will be pure and strong in your sleep, in your lost time, and in your spare time. Formulate your conceptions and marry them with what you have. The combination will bring love and joyous surprises to your life each and every day. Beautiful and joyous experiences are the consequence of pure, genuine, and wonderful thoughts about the good that is in your life. Continue with these thoughts and more joy will be brought into your life's experiences.

A man with a vision will one day be that which he sees, just as a man without a vision will surely perish. Do not give up your vision or your dreams for anything. Cultivate your dreams and goals and show them off to anyone who crosses your path. People will not understand your vision or dreams all the time, but that is alright. The more people that know your vision can help you to achieve it. The more you think about what you will one day be, the closer you come to being that person. The more you dream, the shorter your difficult days will become, and the sooner you will start to enjoy them. Because of the short time it will take you to achieve your dreams, you will have a lot more life to enjoy them. So Aim high and shoot often!!

How To Turn Luck To Your Favor with a short prayer
"My Boundless Knowledge with the assistance of grand wisdom will show what is necessary for me to do. I count on these gifts that I possess to lead me to the fortune that I seek each day, in every way."

This is a prayer that is prayed by those who want to have fortune smile in their direction. This short prayer when prayed on daily and purposefully, will pay out grand dividends to the person who prays. To believe what kind of completely credible, yet seemingly incredible powers are inside us all, is the key to the success of this prayer. We all have the power of God inside of us, as God created us in his own image he did not fail to include the masterful workings of his incredible miraculous powers. These powers are available in our seldom used, yet always present subconscious mind.

God wants us all to be prosperous and happy. He doesn't see fit to have us want for anything. He is always successful and perfect and he wants us all to have the same. So go out in the world and accomplish your desires, really show the world that you are hungry to make a difference. Do not be afraid to shine your good attitude and powerful personality in the direction of those who stand in the way of making things happen in your favor.

God gives us the right of free will, so some can, and may, choose to use that gift to corrupt the great and incredible powers of their mind and body. But God wants us to be successful and if God be with us, who can be against us? Being successful is your great privilege and honor, but free will and weakness of mind will sometimes override success by suffocating the belief that you can accomplish everything you set out to do. When you don't have faith that you can do what you set out to do, you essentially cause ruin to the power of Boundless Knowledge, whose purpose is to show you how you can manage to become successful in all that you want. A defeatist mindset labors to lay waste to an energetic and unfailing power.

Give up the defeatist mindset in every aspect of your life and let the bountiful gifts that your Lord has given you shine through to the hearts and minds of all people in this world. This is where God's work is surely done.

Remember The Simple Law Of Life

The law of life is the law of belief. A man is as he thinks. This law challenges you to think of benevolence, success, happiness, health and all the great gifts that this life has to offer us. With thoughts of these wonderful gifts being regularly impressed upon your mind, these things will surely come to you. This is the greatness of the law of life.

Think of good things and they will come to you. This does not mean that you don't have to act to achieve. The thought is the first step and the most powerful step in the process of getting where you want to be. The next step is also up to you. A man with all the luck in the world can not win the lottery if he doesn't buy a ticket. You need to act, but the thoughts are the impetus; the thoughts are the energy that drive all your endeavors and help you to attain all your dreams and goals.

All good things will come to those who are patient and perseverant. All of life is not lived for instant gratification, although there is a lot of that, it is far better for your health and well-being to work in a direction to attain the things you want, than to have them become yours by cheating the natural process in some way. Patience is an unused commodity in today's society, yet those who learn to use it are able to shape their lives in a manner to which they are very pleased and satisfied.

Please Understand:

***Man's accomplishments, joys, and agonies are all the essence of what they think.

***What you believe in your true heart is what matters.

***Your perception of what you will one day be, is what all others will one day see in you.

***To draw out the good in all bad situations is the essence of existence and shows your strength.

***Every issue and challenge that you come across can be outperformed by you, who is in the form and function of the Heavenly Father.

***You are the temple through which God works his divine plan. Knowing this will help you to believe that your failures are not God's will, because God never fails and would not wish failure on you.

What You Believe Causes Your Experiences

What you believe is the only cause in your world. There is nobody that can change or dictate what occurrences you have in your life. The experiences that develop around you are precipitated by you and maintained by you. The good that you think and believe causes good happenings and the bad thoughts precipitate evil or bad occurrences. You will find that when you begin to shower all your thoughts with good, benevolence, justness, satisfaction, and wellness, your life will grow into a wild new experience for you. Your days will be filled with happenings based on and compounded by the thoughts that you called upon in your mind.

The Life Force, made up of such great gifts as boundless knowledge, healing powers, and endless, unconditional love, are the wonderful capabilities in the form of talents that God has given you on this earthly plane. The ability of your mind is there for you when you call upon it, therefore you must teach it how to respond to your wants and needs. You need to exercise your Life Force and the powers that it harbors, so the response to you is immediate and full of impact when you call upon it. You want your Life Force to communicate with you clearly and succinctly so you can act out what it plans for your life.

Your mind always has the answers that may not at first, or ever, seem abundantly clear. You must train your mind to work in a way that is most fashionable for you. It will work very hard for you once you teach it to search inside you, instead of longing for the outside world to deliver you the answers and guidance. The answer may be delivered up by your mind in the realm of the physical world, but the source to find the answer is always inside you. Be strong and realize with faith and patience, that you have all power inside you to make the answers come.

Focus your thoughts and your energies and strike down all outside interference. Go about acting upon your answer with all of the power, strength, focus, and energy that you can muster. Make the accomplishment swift and definitive, so everyone can see that you possess an amazing amount of might as an individual in all aspects of your life. You have this and are able to use your wonderful inner strength, through the power of the Lord.

Don't Let Anybody Stand In Your Way

Oftentimes people will come to you and ask you what you were thinking making a decision like you did, or taking action in the manner you did. You must stay strong and not let this trivial outside interference affect your decision or action in any way. Your decisions and actions, if thought about and prayed upon will always be right, whether or not it is popular with others who are entwined in your life. All of your energy comes from you. Others' thoughts, words, and deeds will not have any effect on your decisions. You, as a Temple of God, act for God and all other interference has no bearing on your life. Never let outside factors affect the decisions in which you have faith.

Count on and take strength in your faith in God. God's power will enable you to overcome all fear, worry, and the dangers that might otherwise sway you in a direction that is not of your best choosing. Don't let the winds of confusion isolate you from the island of decision. The God power within you has the ability like no other, to keep you in the realm of your Boundless Knowledge which will never leave you in despair or longing. Count on these gifts to guide you through, and the answer that comes is the right answer.

One Thing You Can Always Count On

Just as all things always change and appear like fluid motion in one very large universe, so to should our ideals and convictions. We have to be open to the changes that take place in this world. Man has always believed that steel is solid, but in reality, now that we can see down to molecules and smaller, we find that steel is a mass of very fluid, closely connected molecules that make it look solid in our world. In the world of microcells and microorganisms, steel is porous. Politics change everyday, person-to-person, event-to-event, and word-by-word. What is suitable one day is not suitable and acceptable the next. People living in today's time need to understand that we too must change to meet with these changing conditions on a moment's notice.

We must keep our minds open to change, and ponder, think, and meditate the changes. Then, when we understand how we fit into, or how we can affect those changes, we do what we need to do as free thinking and free-willed individuals. Just as these things are true, people must look at the changes inside themselves and discover what powers are brimming and ready to be displayed. People then must have confidence in these powers and use them because they are the energy that through use and display, leads people to the proper paths of life. It is these energies that clearly define and accentuate each person individually. This power that each man possesses, when connected with the power of other people, forms cohesiveness in community. This energy also affects world events and provides for the changes in culture that are necessary as people progress through the ages.

If you are finding it difficult to call upon peace, you can't sleep at night, or feel inferior, you will not be able to search outside of yourself for wealth, security, success, and happiness. You need to understand that all of these pieces are all part of our life puzzle. As we have a life puzzle, we also have the pieces to put the puzzle of life together on our own without the help or guidance of anyone else. You have to know that God put inside of you all the pieces of the puzzle that you need to solve, you just need to find them and figure out where they belong. A simple assignment when you focus and draw forth the power from within. Be sure to analyze the situation and patiently draw upon the correct piece that gives you satisfaction and happiness.

The fastest and most efficient way to find them is to have faith that the pieces are there. The next step would be to understand through the Boundless Knowledge that is gathered up inside of you, that to operate the mind requires understanding of the laws of the mind. The laws of the mind don't care what you look like, what you sound like, what you smell like, or how suave or debonair you are. The laws of the mind operate on a simple scientific premise just like any of the sciences such as Physics, or Mathematics.

The "A" number one law is that whatever is impressed on the subconscious mind is acted out by the subconscious mind. Simply stated to put this all into perspective; what you reap is what you sow. If you base the workings of your mind on science, if you practice and study it, you will soon understand that what you practice, you become good at, just like the sciences and sports. Two-hundred lay-ups per day with each hand will make any basketball player better on the fast-break. Two-hundred good things of any nature fed into your mind each day will make any human better. The same principle, the same results. The law contained in this science is not difficult to understand, but when you're not used to it, it can be difficult to put into practice. Practice does make perfect, and it builds memory by which you can more quickly call upon it in situations in the future.

The great secret to having everything you want in life should not really be any great secret and I firmly believe that there are very many successful people in this world who know these secrets, because without them there can not be success. I also believe there is enough success, and wealth, and happiness for every man to have 1,000 times more than enough to satiate him. It is this simple belief that sets me out to show everyone how to achieve such things. It is these people on whom I have based my studies, and it is these people that have made it possible for you to have this book so you can discover the secrets that they have known in their families for generations.

Your God Given Powers Are Within You!!

It is time to start invigorating and burning the fire within you, so you can bring back to life the powers that were so hot inside you at birth. It is time to take the lead role in your life and set yourself up to achieve those dreams you have, and start to put together a plan that will get you where you want to be. God has placed every ounce of his spirit in everyone and he expects you to use this as one of your talents to achieve the goals that you set for yourself. The God that created you does not fail and does not believe in failure, so there is no excuse as you unravel the secrets to working with the power of your mind and unleashing your God given power, that you can't achieve anything you set out to do. Achievement is based on your thoughts, so the belief that you can accomplish something puts you firmly into a position to accomplish it.

Prepare a list of goals and dreams on a sheet of paper and set it before you. This list should contain at least six items that you want to accomplish, or six areas of your life that you want to fix, or a combination of the two. When you get that list of accomplishments made up of victories that you would like to have, set it before you and memorize it. When it is memorized put it into a safe place where you will be able to refer to it or show it to people. This list is a reminder that you are not satisfied with your lot in life and would like to do and have more. List-making is a common practice in life and is what keeps people striving to accomplish and perform.

After you have taken those two steps in the right direction, pray in a way that will set those dreams into reality. Something like this:

"My God is my Father and as his son he has given me all power to succeed at everything I choose. His guidance leads me on the path to fulfillment and I am successful in every aspect that leads me to the attainment of my goals".

Pray this prayer every morning and every night before bed. That is two times in your day that you will be feeding your mind good things. Praying on this prayer for one month's time will bring about profound and dramatic change that I have seen in many instances. If after some time you are not seeing a difference, then change the wording of the prayer to suit your specific needs.

An Effort To Break Free From All Your Troubles

Don't believe that the world has any power over you or can make things happen to you. You are the only master of your universe and as master of your universe you decide what holds you back and what draws you ahead. You decide what troubles you, and what challenges you will overcome. Nobody, no matter what position or post, or message being sent, has the ability to command any power over you. Believe in yourself and your God-given powers so you can show others that you are not around to be manipulated by their ideals and wants. You have your own ideals and will work toward them. The Laws of your mind are the true and dependable sources that you can refer to whenever it seems that life has given you a difficult position. Be completely confident in these laws and you will feel the overwhelming presence of your God in your heart.

Your God-given powers have been bestowed upon you and remain inside of you. You need to use these powers to overcome all of your fears and troubles. You need to rise up inside yourself by using your God-given powers and take charge of your life. When you use your natural God-given powers you will find that your troubles and fears were just veils of confusion and temporary misdirection. You will use your abilities to cut down these hills of confusion and take back control of your life with a clear picture of what you need to do next.

You Can Have All The Things You Want

When you're willing to pay the price, it is possible, probable, and given, that you can have anything you want. The price to pay is decided by you. And the results of your want will always satisfy you. What's more, the results will often surprise and amaze you. You must forget man's unwritten rule that if it sounds too good to be true it is, because if you want something and really believe that you can have it, you will get it. Faith is the catchall to attaining your wants, without it you have nothing, but with it you have everything.

Increase Your Ability To Have Your Dreams Come True

With faith all things are possible. In the absence of faith no desire is fulfilled. These two statements are true, but how can you increase your faith so you can have all your dreams come true? The laws of the mind are certain and able to be exercised by all people. You can grow in faith by nurturing your mind and providing it with the nutrients that make it grow and flourish. Like a child who plants a seed, waters it, gives it sun, talks to it, and provides soil for it, you will reap the rewards of your mind by spending the necessary time feeding and tending to it.

When you want a particular tangible or intangible benefit in your life, or the conclusion of a particular struggle, you must first impress upon your mind through clear visualization, what it is that you want, this is the planting stage. Then you must tend to the idea. You have to work with and nurture all aspects of the idea, then you have to be patient and watch for the answer. The benefit, or change that you receive, will unravel and develop into exactly the idea that you had planted in your mind. You have to be patient and you have to be faithful because it is with patience and faith that the answers will come and your life will take on the changes that you visualize.

There are many successful people in this world, very successful people, too many to mention. They are all of different backgrounds and have made their accomplishments a reality through their diligence, patience, and faith. Faith, is attention paid to a particular idea or subject. Meditation and focus are key objects of faith and must be used to clearly identify what you seek. When you stick to the ideal to which you have strengthened your faith, you will accomplish that end.

When you are confident in your ability to bring about the results, your subconscious will use the energies that you have amassed through your focus, to bring about the results you seek. Always stay true to the ideal you have focused on. Keep your nose to the grindstone, and never lose faith. If you can ride high in faith and keep your focus, then your life's accomplishments will be in your complete and total control.

You Can't Lose If You Use This Logic.

The thoughts that you think in your mind can be good or bad. The good create opportunity for quality experiences, general excitement, and accomplishment. The bad thoughts, on the other hand, rob you of all opportunity of accomplishment, excitement, or positive experiences. Providing faith, focus, meditation, and all manners of positive and specifically targeted quality thoughts, are the few keys it takes to provide success in all aspects of your life. The role of faith in the process of creating a life free of struggles and filled with harmony can not be stressed enough, yet more than likely this is the first piece of logic that is forgotten.

Negative mental thoughts, self criticism, or the belief in the verity of criticism by others, is the fastest way to ruin the development of your ideals. Allowing negative thoughts and emotions to set in after the preliminary belief of criticism is the single most destructive path that you can let your ideal take. This is a vile form of self-destruction as you are not placing the faith in the gifts that God gave you. Instead you are permitting others to deceive you and are pulling away from the eternal truth that you control everything in your life. It is important to keep in mind that there is not any outside force which in any way can affect your life, unless you choose to give it the power to do so.

Do not become a victim to cause and effect. Nothing that anyone can say or do can take control of you at any time. You are a child of God, and he hands you autonomy and free-will, this allows you to act and proceed in a manner that is in your best interests. Your interests are inherently unaffected by the words and actions of other people, or any other events or circumstances that occur. Be sure that those things that others say and do are unable to penetrate your thoughts and affect the life that you are making for yourself with the powers of your heart and mind.

All Questions Are Answered

In the event that you have a question, know that the answer lies within the vast workings of your mind. You see, all questions that you find it necessary to ask, already have an answer available to you in your mind. Your God is the presence that dwells within you as spirit, and he makes all knowledge and wisdom known to you. In the Bible it is stated early and often that whatever problem arises God will solve, whatever question is asked, God will answer.

Belief that your God exists in you as part of you, because you are a child of his, is the first step in understanding that he will be there to answer all your questions and lead you in every aspect of your life to your roads of riches. Always remember too, that you have to give to get. A truly fabulous life will not be gained without some payment by the recipient of great gifts.

A Good Prayer for The Assistance Of Boundless Knowledge

"Lord bless me to understand the power and reach of my Boundless Knowledge. Help me to understand how it works and how I need to provide the questions to receive the answers that I seek. Help me to call upon it and focus my energies to receive the answers that come."

You will always find that the solution is within the challenge with which you are faced. In all the times in your life that you come upon a problem or challenge to which you see no immediate solution you should call on the vast temple of knowledge stored up within yourself to find the answer to the challenge. The powers that God bestowed upon you are available in the subconscious mind, and the subconscious mind knows all and sees all. The subconscious never sleeps, never gets tired and never breaks down. The Life Force and the powers that dwell in it, without fail, are always there for you. When you have a problem or challenge that you can not see a clear and vivid solution to, look within yourself and your omnipresent powers that God bestowed upon you, and you will see clear to the answer and solution to that problem.

All you need to do is call upon the powers that God gave you, and he will give you assurance and guidance to see you through to the successful resolution of your problems.. Inside you is a vast and complex network of problem solving ability which I like to call your Boundless Knowledge. This system is available and working for you day and night. This is the system that causes you to find the answer to the problem or question while you sleep or drift off to think of something else. Once you pose a question to your mind that you can not readily answer on your own in the conscious state, the subconscious mind starts to use its incredibly vast amount of resources to search and seek out the answer. If you feel you want that answer, your subconscious mind will find it for you and make it readily understandable to you.

In order for you to find the answers to all the questions that you have and all the challenges that you face, you must learn to tap into the boundless knowledge that is available to you, in a more efficient and effective manner. You must begin to train the mind to do what it does naturally, in a more practical way; to work for you in a way that is most beneficial to you. The way to do that is to study and learn the way your Boundless Knowledge proceeds now, and channel it to work in a way that allows you to access the answers more quickly and deliberately. The method you can use to bring this about is giving your Life Force a workout on a regular basis. The more you use the life Force and the powers contained within, the more readily accessible these powers will become to you. Finding your true God-given powers requires meditation and focus; it requires patience and faith, and dedication to your overall plan.

You must truly want to attain that which you set out to accomplish. If you want to have sweeping changes in your life, you have to truly and steadfastly want them. You have to thirst for these changes, and know in full that these changes are going to be one-hundred percent what you want. Your decision must be final and your buy-in must be complete. Anything short of complete buy-in about your decision will cause dissonance in your subconscious mind. Your Boundless Knowledge will not know whether it needs to work on bringing about the new, changed you, or sticking with the old you that you feel comfortable with at the current time.

The old adage "Change your mind to change your life" is as true now as it ever was. But this change is not whether or not you are going to rake the lawn today. No, this change is the most dramatic change that you could call on Boundless Knowledge to perform for you. This change will take you from your current self with tons of unused potential to the new you that has abilities, and uses them efficiently and effectively. The changed you exudes confidence and draws from the strength within to accomplish the goals that are set in your mind. This being the case, you can not drone out a few lines of affirmation each morning before a mirror, believing that with constant repetition your life's path will be reformulated. This will never work; the buy-in is not sincere and the want is not truly there.

All your abilities are in you already. These talents are always available to you no matter what your need is. If you desire something to make your life better or more complete, then call upon the power of the Life Force to attain what you want. These are the talents that are God-given, but you have to use them in order for them to blossom back into the gifts with the full potential you were born with. The lack of use of your Life Force since birth has unfortunately caused it to get buried deep down in the mind, but this can be remedied and brought right back to the top of mind with increasing regular use.

For you to reap the unlimited rewards of your subconscious mind, you must call upon these powers often and exercise them. You have to take each day as it comes and see how that day and its challenges fit into your picture of what you want your life to be like. You must challenge the subconscious mind by focusing yourself on a goal and calling upon your Boundless Knowledge to lead you to that goal. Whatever you ask of your Boundless Knowledge will be given to you, short of evil or devious ends. Have faith and a good attitude, and then you can surely rest in the fact that your Boundless Knowledge will present to you a plan of action to overcome whatever troubles you currently see before you. When necessary, your Life Force will lift the haze of confusion that exists in your mind, that causes you to see and dwell upon the bad parts of your life instead of the good.

I have read, and been told the stories many times, about people who are not happy in their lives. These people are able to turn their lives around and make a new and fresh start of it. The greatest accomplishment that any person can have is taking the life that they find to be without purpose or meaning, or the life that is just not quite what they had planned for themselves, and turning it into the life that they had always dreamt of having. The common denominator that I find in all of these stories is that they could not have done it without the power of God in their lives.

They all say that having God in their lives is the reason and the resolve in bringing their true lives to fruition. These stories are truly amazing and I marvel at the complexities and challenges that they were able to overcome, but truly everyone has the ability to perform such miraculous life recoveries. God gave everyone incredible powers and he has made them available to you if you just believe.

What people with life-changing stories don't say, but I find out later in conversations with them is that they felt a power unlike anything they had ever felt before, working inside of them. The power was like a light, or a glow. It was a burning desire! This burning desire is a blessing that God gives to people when they call on the gifts that he has bestowed upon them to help them through the rough times that come their way. God incites a volcano of power, a hurricane of motivation, and a lifetime of strength, to assist you every time you call on him and the majestic, omnipotent, power that he has given you.

Boundless Knowledge is one of those gifts, and its powers are unmatched by the largest and fastest supercomputers. Its vast amount of energy, insight, power, and will, is inexplicable and unfathomable. We know it exists because the books of religion, prophets, and our hearts tell us it is there. It's there in all beauties beyond description and it is waiting for you to tap into its amazing truth.

Life's Challenges Can Be Overcome!

Just remember that the challenges that life sends your way are not really challenges from the game of life, rather they are perceived challenges from you. Life and the obstacles that stand in your way are part of the way you think and view the world. You know in your heart that there is nothing outside of you that affects the way you do things. Nothing affects the way you accomplish your daily and life goals. All power to overcome is within you and all obstacles are within you. Your oversight of your God-given power is what draws conclusions making you feel that you don't control every aspect of your life.

If God is with you, who can be against you? This is a question that you should ask yourself whenever you are feeling that all odds are insurmountable or ominous. This question draws out the answer that is prefaced by the fact that God is always there and always knowing. Every minute of every day, God is your wingman. Don't fail to be all you can be, because of a lack of confidence that leaves you afraid to stand in front of your peers and say "I can do this." You should be confident all the time because God has got your back.

There is no fear, no heartache, no sorrow, and no anger in the house where God dwells. If you feel that you have been living a life somewhat out of your control, you have to put faith back into your life. Focus, and faithfully observe whatever challenges you, this will demonstrate for you just what your challenge is to you. In this process of demonstration you will see just how to find the weaknesses in the challenge, giving you full knowledge of what it takes to overcome it.

You will find that in all cases, your fear, obstacle, or challenge is imaginary. Delving deeper to the root of the challenge will reveal that your fear is what you believe the challenge could ultimately become. Due to the fact that the challenge is your perception of what it could amount to, but certainly is not, you must develop an ability to neutralize emotions from all negative past experiences. There is no threat that the challenge can bring to you without your remembrance of past experiences. Work on negating all past negative and traumatic experiences, and your perceptions that currently scare you will no longer bring you fear.

When you find yourself to be fearful of the thoughts that you make of situations, relax in the knowledge that with your faith you can proclaim that there is no fear where faith in God resides. All fears can fall into the haze of disbelief, when you understand that the power of God that resides in you, can push away all your trepidation with one swoop. Take on projects in your personal life or at work that you would normally feel afraid to take, and face those fears with the power of God. You will surely overcome your fears and succeed at the project.

With faith in providence you should continue to explore the powers of your subconscious mind and the very powerful thoughts that dwell inside. In your exploration you will conceivably uncover powers of prosperity and abundance, the power to heal, the incredible power to forgive, and the powers that you hold to bring happiness to your life. These incredible powers are alive inside all people, but very few ever stop to consider them, fewer yet ever use them.

A Very Special Person

I was talking with a man one day whom I had met, that I thought to be homeless. He was one of the most pleasant people I had ever met. The man was talking about how he became homeless. He had a very good paying and prestigious job, his kids were grown, and his wife had passed away. He had done everything in his life that he had planned for himself to do. He had a dream house, he put his children through college, he had vast amounts of wealth both in the form of material possessions and bank accounts, as well as the relationships that he had developed and nurtured with many people.

I asked him why he was now homeless. He answered "a man who doesn't have a home is not necessarily homeless." He slept on the streets in some towns, alleys in other towns. He slept on a park bench sometimes. He was always moving on, walking from town to town or hitchhiking to get from one place to another. This man had told me that in some towns where he had a lot of friends, if the weather was not in cooperation, he would call on a friend to put him up, and they always did. Now when his friends put him up, they also put up any friend he had along with him on the streets. Sometimes he had one friend, sometimes many.

I asked in amazement how his affluent friends felt about taking in total strangers and he explained to me that the relationship that he had with his affluent friends lent him quite a bit of lenience in the standard rules of their house. He had friends for years that would take him in and they always said that if he cared enough to befriend them, then they were good enough to stay in the house in their company too. This man had the respect, trust, and loyalty of his affluent friends and the respect, trust, and loyalty of his street friends.

Such a marriage of company would not be looked upon as too ordinary under normal circumstances. This man told me that after all his accomplishments and success in the world earning money and impressing people, he needed to use his natural born abilities for a new and extraordinary challenge that would bring his life into true focus. It was that day that he gave all he had away, and began to establish relationships with a crowd that he hadn't ever had the propensity to meet. His desire was to make friends with people that had little to nothing in the way of earthly possessions, so he could learn what their driving force was. He wanted to find out what made and kept them content with no material possessions.

He used his power of Boundless Knowledge to understand how to interact with the people of the streets and how to survive and enjoy life as a homeless person. All of life's challenges at this point had been overcome through the power of his subconscious mind and his Boundless Knowledge within. A new challenge was ripe with promise for him and he was desiring to enjoy what this new life would bring. He looked happy and healthy, although a little dirty, and was as focused on his new life as I could ever believe he was in his past life.

He told me that he had never had a more enjoyable living than his life on the street. All the fancy cars, clothes, and homes that he had in the past, meant nothing. Enjoying life with nothing was the way to go. Never any worries, never any deadlines. Nobody calling in favors, none of the rat race. This truly was a man who had fulfilled a desire, unaffected by the thoughts and actions of others. Back then, I was a little frightened of him, but now I look back in great fondness of what he had accomplished and how happy he had become.

Without the knowledge and use of his God-given higher powers, he would have had no idea how to interact with the people of the streets, nor would he have known that he could have complete happiness with this life. I told him that he was a testament to the amazing power and wonder of Boundless Knowledge. He was a testament to all the powers of God that reside within all people when we choose to see them and unleash the incredible power. He asked me to join him for a couple of days on the streets. I am still not ready for that lifestyle.

Business Is Slow!!

How do I overcome a challenge in the way of my business not thriving? This was a question I was asked one time by a businessman that I knew. I was caught off guard at first by the question, but then I started to ask him some questions. The business he was in was metal fences. He was a distributor and installer and had some really keen competition with an old high school rival. After several questions about the competition all ending in defaming remarks about his old high school rival, I quickly learned that this man had so much stored up animosity and resentment that it was impossible for him to see his business mission and service clearly. He seemed to be spending four to five hours a day dreaming up deceptive ways to run his old rival out of business instead of working with his customers, assuring quality, and following up with customer service calls, a simple courtesy that in itself would boost sales and referrals.

I told my friend that demand for this product is ferocious. It seems that everyone in a three state area with any kind of property wants to buy this product. I explained to him that his sales were slumping because instead of spending his quality and valuable time working on securing his customer base and all the benefits that come with that, he was spending his time in a pool of resentment and animosity that was self destructive. I explained to him that in order to get anything you want in life, you have to want it bad. You have to desire it enough to give up something, sometimes something very near and dear. In this case his animosity and resentment are the two things that he had to release to receive his blessings. His God-given talents in this case were working against him, not because he had wanted them to, but because God wants us all to love one another. His animosity and resentment and intention to harm another human being was going against the principles and laws of our subconscious mind which are to protect and act in a benevolent manner.

Soon after this talk, my friend conceded and withdrew his resentment and his business immediately surged to new levels of sales and service. This is a testament to the wonderful healing and righteous powers of our subconscious mind. It was clear to me what the problem was, because I know how the subconscious mind operates. The subconscious mind is not different person to person or on a case by case basis. The subconscious mind and the power of Boundless Knowledge operates on laws and principles. Laws and principles never vary. The only variance comes in the way you use your powers and for what you use them. A great prayer to forgive old bitterness and help to gain prosperity and happiness goes like this:

"God's love and good will floods my heart and mind. I will pour forth good will and love to all those around me and all people everywhere for their own device. If I have any ill feelings toward any person I will draw them out and pray for their prosperity, healing, guidance, and forgiveness. I will continue to do this until I can meet and greet this person without any negative feelings."

You can alter this with your preferred vocabulary. Focus on this prayer two times per day and work on forgiving others for things you perceive they have done wrong to you, or others. Don't let yourself fall into the same trap. Pour out blessings upon others and pray for their accomplishment and success. The rewards will come back upon you many times over.

The World Is Inundated With Cause And Effect

Do not be consumed by the outside world. Do not be affected in any way by the imaginary powers of the outside world. And don't let the outside world enter into your thoughts. The outside world that we see on a daily basis that may look mean, cruel, and callous, is the conglomeration of all the causes that all men have. The way the outside world looks to you is the effect, and all men are the cause. Do not let the perceived effect of the outside world pervade your personal dreams and goals. Be steadfast to your dreams and goals because they will surely affect the outside world, and in time, have people change their ideals to be more in tune with yours.

Start Your Own Ripple Effect

The world is cause and effect. Cause is the fundamental power that drives the world through man's thoughts. Man, in his mind has a cause which is an ideal or a value, a dream or a goal. This cause is passed on in his quest to attain fulfillment of his cause, which is effect. This creates a ripple effect; a very small amount of mass (energy of a thought) enters the huge pool of human effort, thought, and action, and begins to make a very slight difference. People do however see this difference. They see the ripple, and often times many people enjoy the ideal which caused the ripple. This can affect their thoughts, ideals, or personal cause to resemble your cause. Soon more people do the same and this effectively shifts the perception of the outside world. All this comes about with the power of just one positive thought at a time.

The shift of the perception of the outside world after each additional thought seems to more resemble your original ideal. You take away great confidence from this happening (which again is your perception of the outside world). Soon all ideals that you have are free flowing to the world cause and the world cause is starting to take on the form of your very original and authentic ideal. Follow this chain with me for a moment for this is the model of how the world formulates the conglomeration of cause and ideals.

1) Starts with a thought, ideal, or value
2) The ideal causes a ripple in the pre-existing conglomeration of ideas which is solely based on our perception of how the world is operating and changing (for the good or the bad).
3) Others begin to perceive the ripple.

4) Others start to become affected by the ripple and align their ideals more closely to yours.
5) They begin to share your ideals creating more ripples onto the pool of effect.
6) Soon the small ripple that you set forth is the face in the pool of effect.
7) Your ideal being good and just and widely accepted, lets you grow in confidence to set free more ideals for the world to accept or reject based on their ideals and the perception which makes up their reality.

Your ideals are personally yours. You must make a deep connection to them so that they can take on the characteristics that you want them to represent on the world screen. Let all of your old perceptions and outdated ideals and thoughts fall off the face of the earth. There is no reason to believe in the evils and corrupt ideals of the world, because on the world screen, billions of thoughts and ideas will be passed, and you can choose which ones you want to make up your perception of the world. Perception is reality, if the sky looks blue to you on a cloudy day, then the sky is blue. Choose wisely that which makes up your reality, because this is what you will see all the time. You wouldn't rather see the cloudy gray sky than the blue sky, would you?

Life Just Keeps Getting Better.

The fact that you are alive and well and reading this book is pure ecstasy. This means that you are a person who can think for yourself and you enjoy thought provoking subjects that assist you to bring out your inner wonder, beauty, and power. But, have you ever contemplated the vast array of wonders stored up inside of you? You are a child of God and God lives through you. This means that all those wonderful abilities, talents, and powers that are inside of you that I have alluded to, throughout this book, are available to you. Not only that, but even greater wonders that we have not touched upon yet are available to you as well.

These wonders available inside of you through the power of God, are just waiting for you to call upon them. You will use them in a manner in which they were destined to perform, amaze, and inspire you. All of this available power is fit to perform such a function in your life that just knowing of your God-given abilities, will lead you to accomplishments that you have long dreamt about. By the end of this book, I will have done a very good job of introducing you to your God-given powers and giving you examples of what you are capable of when you put them to use. What this book will not have done however, is completely inform you of your personal power that was given to you. Although everyone has the same gifts and talents of God inside of them, for each person, the tasks and feats performed will be different. For each person, the tasks and feats you accomplish will be amazing and awe-inspiring in your own personal way.

Zeal and desire are the main driving forces behind all accomplishments. You need to desire and have a zeal or passion for what it is that you want before your inner wonders can begin to express themselves in a way that will lead you to the achievement you have in mind. Most people desire to have a great relationship with a spouse and with all their loved ones. I am sure that you desire to be healthy, happy, and live in a nation where you have the freedom to express yourself in the manner you choose. I feel confident that you have a passion to prosper towards great wealth, doing what you love to do. Passion, zeal, and desire are behind all advancement and accomplishment in everything. Without one of these driving forces, which not incidentally, are all connected, you will not succeed, prosper, advance, or lead.

The Life Force breathes life into all of us and makes us who we are. The Life Force also has a desire, it desires to express and experience itself. As plants and trees desire to grow, as wild animals desire to run, and as a flower desires to blossom, you too desire something. Is that desire prosperity, a long healthy life, security, or happiness? Whatever you desire, the fact that you desire it will drive you toward your goal. That's what desire does, its passion alone pushes you, drives you, even forces you to do the things you know you must do to attain that which you desire (your goal). This is the influence of the Life Force and it always accomplishes that which you truly desire.

Your passions keep you on the road to accomplishment in your life. Accomplishments, that when completed will have made your life a more complete and pleasant journey, are ultimately the pieces of your life that others will remember. The greater the happiness and excitement for the enrichment in your life, the stronger the passion will be. When you don't expect enrichment from an accomplishment you will not act on it and your Life Force will not act to assist you in acquiring it. You must expect and have faith that your passion will drive your Life Force to accomplishment in all that you do.

Frustration and unhappiness will ensue when over a long period of time you fail to actualize your desires. The Life Force, which is a gift from God, is here to assist you in finding happiness and prosperity. Your passion for a given life enrichment assists you in being able to say that you choose it for the good it will bring to your life. Make sure you choose what benefits you would like for your life. Make your goals big and really want them, and you will achieve success in each one.

Do Not Suppress Your Desires

Over the years, I have seen many people suppress desire. I even tried it for a period of a few months while I was experimenting with one of the very exclusive religious sects I was studying. I found that suppressing my desires made me to be a rigid automaton who always did what I was told to do at every moment of my days. The mere suggestion that I should do something for myself or for someone else led me to action towards that end. It was crazy.

Before I had started that excruciating experiment, I had read that it is a devastating blow to the mind and body to behave in a manner that suppresses your desires. I had no feeling of want and no feeling of pain, regret, sadness, anger, happiness or any other emotion that one might be subject to on a daily basis. I am sure to bystanders, family, and friends, it was like a life of evil. I thought prior to the experiment, that the only affect such an experiment would have would be that I wouldn't want anything, and I would live my life happily as a minimalist. That wasn't the case.

I also had more trouble drawing myself out of the wretched state than I had proposed at the outset of the experiment. Thankfully, somehow, I still had access to the all powerful God-given powers within me. I was able to muster up the strength and wonder, to pour out upon me the great gifts of life. Even though I had not called upon the powers of my Life Force that God had given me, and I suppressed all desires which drive the Life Force, the powers God gave me were still there waiting for me to call upon them. If I had been in a commune behaving in that manner for that period of time, I am not sure that I would have come out of it.

Desire, as I stated earlier, is a vital and integral part of life. The lack of desire takes away your ability to make choices. Without a desire to participate in one job instead of another, one relationship instead of another, or one hobby instead of another, you would be living a supreme disappointment from what life is supposed to be. In this way of living there is no free will, because choices are nonexistent. You do what you are told or make decisions without a process of thought about how it will affect your life, either positively or negatively. Desire is what causes all feeling and action and is a necessary part of human life. You wouldn't take the oil out of your car engine, in like manner, you shouldn't take the desire out of your heart.

Your desire is one more thing, it is a creative power that works through you. This power of creativity is astonishingly complex and differs immensely from person to person. Desire is also part of what makes individual expression so unique and interesting. No two people will ever choose all the same paths in life. No two people will ever make all the same decisions, and no two people will ever dance the same dance in expression of their creative power. These expressions, in the form of choices or the arts, are the communication of the desires and ideals of our minds to the outside world. The color car we drive, and the speed at which we drive it are just two more examples of choices made either consciously or subconsciously. These choices are pieces that move us sometimes unknowingly toward our ultimate goals in expression of our individual ideals.

The Power Of Desire

To desire is natural and healthy. If you are poor, you desire to have abundance or be rich; If you are sick, you desire to be healthy, and if you are dejected and forgotten, you desire forgiveness and love. To desire is to long for the fulfillment of a basic need. Even above basic needs desire is healthy, as whatever you attain through desire helps you to become more of who you are. Desire helps you to paint a picture for the world to see all the good that comes when you call upon your God-given powers of the Life Force.

You have to be careful not to misinterpret desire, because breaking the law or your own moral code to fulfill your desire will leave you in a lot of trouble. For instance, you and your spouse are having marital problems from a lack of communication. You desire affection and you know the neighbor is home and cares for you. Don't believe that you should go to your neighbor for affection. Instead, turn to your spouse and open the lines of communication, offer up love and affection and you will get the same in return. The Boundless Knowledge within you can fulfill every desire; call on it, and the answers will be given to you. A prayer that will fuel your desires and assist you in attaining whatever you desire:

"My Father and I are in like mind. I have my being in him and he lives in me. He knows my every desire and graces me with Boundless Knowledge and the Life Force within to make wise decisions and accomplish all

I set out to do. Love is given to me freely, Health is poured out upon me from within, and Peace fills my heart with warmth and comfort."

Do you know what the Life Force is and what it means to you? The Life Force is a gift from God, and God is the Life Force. God has sent down his spirit as the Life Force that works within you to sustain you. Having the faith to trust in God builds confidence in yourself, in your wisdom, intelligence, and power. It gives you confidence and is the inverse of inferiority, ignorance, stupidity, and cowardice.

If you are at a point in your life right now where you feel that everything is against you, you can't get ahead, only the rich get richer, and only those who are able to work out all the time are healthy, then you are suffering without reason. You need to understand that whatever you ask for will be given to you. You need to realize that what you want to do, you can do, what you want to be, you can be. You need to perceive that all the life that you want is attainable. There is no cruel fate of the world around you that condemns you to a life of unhappiness, mediocrity or poverty. The Life Force works to help you set your fate on the riches of the earth, betterment of society, and the sharing of love.

Go After It!

The world is your oyster and you have to snap up what you want when it becomes available to you. Don't let the wilds of the world deter you from taking from this world what you desire to take. All that you see when you look out your window is your perception of the world. It is not the truth unless you accept it as truth and ground your faith to it. I have to tell you though, that there is no evil plot that sentences you to any of the misery, deprivation, poverty, or loneliness that you perceive in the world. So if you are tired of these things, then change your reality. Change your mind and you change your life. Rid yourself of false beliefs that you have built up throughout the years, shake off the terrible impressions that are tattooed to your mind. You can do it! Here is a prayer that works to rid yourself of your preconceived notions, prejudiced viewpoints, and inability to see the world in the light of day:

"Lord shine down your light upon my mind and break me free from the unstable effects of the negativity that invades my mind and holds me to captive thoughts of doom and gloom."

It is the wrong thought to believe that you need to be a prisoner of want, enslaved to trepidation, a hostage to anger, imprisoned by loneliness, or in bondage to hate. You are an individual with the rights and privileges of free-will, therefore you have the opportunity to turn all things in a different direction at any time. There is nothing holding you back, and nobody making your decisions for you, so the time is now to release this bondage to your perceived captors and send your negative thoughts out of the realm of your reality.

The Lord Wants You To Shine Like A New Dime

All decisions and all direction is given by you and for you. There is nobody that holds any power over you, so the lot that you are now in, is your chosen lot whether you want to accept it or not, it is the truth. All of the problems, strains, and breaks in your life, be it spiritual, physical, or mental are brought on by the thoughts of your mind. Don't attempt any longer to blame anyone else for your troubles or fears. God is not responsible, neither are your parents, nor is some secret unknown faction operating with direction from a foreign or local government. The only governor of your mind is the thought and ideal that you feed to it daily. Be sure to feed your mind well, be positive, and look forward to the wonderful opportunities, challenges, and benefits that will come your way from doing so.

Desire is an amazing and powerful gift from God that you can use to attain anything and everything that you want. Feed this hunger to make it large and make it tangible. You need to put a face on your desire, you need to make it so it can be photo-framed, so that your mind has a clear picture for what it is that you hunger. Make your desire beautiful and captivating, have it be your sole purpose by which you spend your days longing and your sleep-filled nights dreaming. Taking your desire to the extreme will give your mind the very clear picture that it is this one desire for which you so hunger, that everything else overtly takes a back seat to it. This will push your desire to the top of your list for the gift of your Boundless Knowledge to begin to act on and fulfill.

Wanting Is Man's Nature, Not A Sin

It is not a sin to not settle with your current lot in life. To want is part of man's nature and to always want what is better for you and your family promotes a bond of trust within the family and lends your mind peace from negative thoughts that sometimes creep in when there is a lull in activity. The wanting is healthy and promotes the positive functioning and ease of use of the faculties that assist the developments of accomplishment and purpose. Fulfilling want and desire is the exercise by which your Life Force and Boundless Knowledge can become stronger, more productive, and efficient. Exercise the powers of your Life Force regularly and often so that its response grows faster and stronger. In time, your mere elementary thoughts will produce a reaction.

Your greatest desire will always be to secure peace of mind. If man is unable to meet his most basic desires such as health, prosperity, and success, he quickly faces disappointment and rage. You need to observe the amazing wonder of your God-given power. Employ this power, majesty, and wonder that is inside of you, to make all your desires come to fruition. This Life Force within you is always present just waiting for you to call upon it with the feeling, want, and desires of your dreams and goals. This power craves to work in you and through you. This power craves for you to fill your desires and show the world on the blank canvas of time and space what you are capable of with the application of your internal Life Force, driven by your deep and full desire.

When you start to exercise God's power, you will begin to feel peace flow through you. You will know and love the fact that the thought processes leading to the convictions that you express to the outside world and your internal consciousness, will lead you to more pure ideals. Your negative thoughts, comments, and views will start to turn away from you. No longer will you find yourself looking at the bad aspects of your life and the world you live in, nor will you so easily find the negative characteristics of your friends, acquaintances, and relatives. Rather, going forward, you will be noticing the wonderful beauties and potentials of each of these groups of people. You will see the world, first on a small scale, growing to a larger scale, exhibit the natural laws of life, love, beauty, and expression that you first started seeing in yourself.

You Have To Give To Get

In order to truly enjoy the wonderful benefits and amazing side-effects of peace of mind, you need to rid your world of your poorly formed perceptions of the life that you currently lead. Far too much of your internal energies, coming from your Life Force that your God has given you, are being used to rid yourself of the worrying and stressing that you do. Using such powerful energies to eliminate the torments that you bring upon yourself needlessly, is a waste of the perfect gifts that you have been given. Even though there is no limit to the amount of Life Force and intelligence that has been bestowed upon you, it is important to always use it for thoughts of benevolence and achievement. Without properly exercising these benefits for the purposes which they were given, you will render them unavailable for their most necessary purpose in your life. You now know that the purpose and function of your talents and blessings is the achievement and accomplishment of all your desires.

You can and should use your inner power of healing to quiet the worries and stresses in your mind that tug at your Life Force. This will calm your concern and help you to focus on your further desires. A prayer to accomplish this end is as follows:

"The perfect law of supply and demand which the Lord sets forth for me, works within me. I am always in touch with whatever I need. The incredible and all powerful healing presence inside me knows what I need to calm myself and give me peace in every situation. The beauty and life of God courses through my veins and I feel and know that he is making me healthy and whole."

Self Assurance Lifts The Veil That Covers Your Eyes

You are a most unique human-being, an extraordinary person in extraordinary times; you have a duty to the world which you may not yet know.

Your duty is to be everything you can be to everyone with which you interact. Your duty is to fully actualize yourself to be all that your Life Force makes it possible for you to be. Your singularity of purpose and your unique approach to life leave you as an individual person with individual thoughts and ideals. Your body is a vessel used to explore and accomplish all that you are capable of at this given time in your life. The God-given powers wish to be expressed and it is your duty in this world to feature those expressions and showcase them in a way which only you are capable.

Use the genius of your individual ideas to draw a picture onto the canvas that is life. Avail yourself to imagination that comes to you in the day and night and use it to create for yourself a life beyond the writings of the greatest authors of all time. Create a story by which the masters of words would blush. All of this possibility is available to you in solid and real form when you let your free-flowing ideals, thoughts, and creativity loose in the world. Throw back the veils that block the sun from your eyes. Open your heart to the many ways that you can make a difference in the world and go out and do what needs to be done. Use the confidence that you possess through your Life Force to make a great impact on all the people around you. Work hard on exercising your internal powers, so people can look and marvel at your accomplishments.

You must understand that you are here for a purpose and it is up to you to fully bring about that purpose by exercising your subconscious mind and all the powers that are made available to you from God.

Your Life Force is bursting in anticipation of what you will become. Your life is to be an individual interpretation to the world of the very unique gifts born inside of you. Your life is to be the adoration of others who long for(but don't know how to bring about) actualization and self-expression.

If You Have Faith, You Have Confidence.

Having faith is the same as having confidence. One of the major benefits of increasing faith in God and the powers that he has given to you, is your confidence and assurance in your abilities is certain to grow. With increased self confidence you are able to face all problems and challenges with vigor. The big challenges of the past will seem smaller and smaller. Faith in your abilities, as you proceed in the knowledge of your gifts, will grow even greater helping you to overcome all obstacles.

Man must have confidence in the Life Force that never abandons him. On your journey, the difficulties will be plentiful and the obstacles substantial. But, unlike those things that tremble and fall, your confidence will continue to stretch, consuming all distractions and roadblocks on the way to the fulfillment of your desires. Be available to God and draw assurance from his availability to you. You are on God's team and God is on yours, with that certitude you will move through all kinds of inconsistency and malady in the world around you with ease.

You are the gift to the Life Force within. Without you, the Life Force has no home and no place through which to work. You are a vessel for the Life Force, and the Life Force is an inspiration for you. Without the Life Force, you would have no purpose whatsoever. You would be the ship without a rudder, the person without vision. The Life Force gives you reason and purpose for living, it helps you create your desires that lead it to act upon those desires. The Life Force is inseparable to you as a fully functioning human being.

Politics, Religion, and Political Agendas are ever-changing in this complex and fast moving world. Earthquakes and volcanoes, hurricanes and tornadoes sometimes destroy towns and halve cities. All things change, all things have their ups and downs, and certainly in the end all things pass away. Your Life Force works contrary to the common laws of man. The laws of the Life Force only grow and generate strength. It is the one thing that you will always be able to count on to be ever-present. The Life Force's only change is that it gets better, bigger, and stronger.

Many people seem to lack confidence due to their lives as children, where they may have lived their lives with dominating and insulting people.. It might have been mom and dad, it may have been an uncle or aunt, it may have been their cohorts at school that filled their heads with insult and ridicule. Whatever reasons people cling to with their inferiority, they have all the power within to reverse the trend and build a life filled with confidence and respect for who they are. These people must desire to let go of the their inferiority.

Sometimes inferiority and lack of confidence becomes a much safer excuse than risking rejection and ridicule later in life. Instead of wanting to draw themselves out and live life with people's acceptance and rejection, they would rather hide away their fragile egos so as not to be hurt in the same manner they were as kids. There are two prayers that I suggest others to pray that will take away all fear of failure, fear of ridicule, and any other fear that keeps people from living their lives in the manner that they should:

"Heavenly love leads me on my path, going out before me to assure that my path is ready for me to journey upon it. It searches for the beauty and joy that it knows I will take comfort in, and leads me through it so I can enjoy the people I meet and have pleasant adventures along the way."

"I am a channel for God's life, love, and wisdom. God my Father is uniquely expressed through me and there is nobody else in all the world like me. God wishes to express himself in an amazing way through me. I am a conduit through which God's power and providence courses. Each day I am able to assert more of my true talents upon the world in which I live."

You are able to do all things through the God-given power of the Life Force that is driven by your desires. You have to believe and know every minute of every day, that the Life Force is with you and longs to be exercised through you. Please desire to be happy, desire to be wealthy, desire to be healthy, and full of joy. It is these desires that will bring all good things into your life. As these gifts are bestowed upon you at an incredible rate, you will notice the difference in the way that you think and act. Negative thoughts will diminish, inferiority will suffer its finest defeat and you will live a life every day filled with the fruits of your God-given gifts.

One of the most imperative pieces of information that you must take away with you is that your subconscious mind is the world where your God-given powers of the Life Force and Boundless Knowledge subsist. Your subconscious mind, which most people don't have a clear understanding of, is the area where all of your power is stored. You must exercise the powers of your subconscious mind through exercises of faith and prayer. You should really get in touch with it by studying your habitual behavior and your habitual thinking. Learn how to impress upon the subconscious all of the necessary elements of the ideal you that you want to portray. Draw out the full power of your Life Force in your subconscious mind by faithfully observing your most fortified desires.

Such exercise in the subconscious mind will provide for strengthened and fortified thoughts and behaviors that separate you from whomever you were before you realized what power was within you waiting to be set free. The life Force is always available to you, all you have to do is call upon it to fulfill your desires and raise your confidence. Call upon it to give you wealth, grant you peace, and still the troubled waters of the world in which you live. It has the power and it will do what you ask, because God and his powers are always with you.

Pass On Your Self Confidence

If you want to fully develop and fine-tune your self-confidence you have to show your faith in the power of the Life Force that lives within you. Exercise it in your subconscious mind through faith and desire. Take all of the successes of your thinking and behavior which you have developed from habit and reinforcement in the promise of the articles it will bring you, and transfer it to your conscious mind. The transfer is of primary importance as it will give you strength in your conscious world as you see the habits shape a new and confident you in your subconscious mind. The anecdotal evidence that your subconscious mind builds, and your conscious mind borrows, is enough to impress upon the conscious mind that the habitual behaviors and thinking have made a difference in the overall you. Your conscious mind quickly catches on because it is driven by fact and logic namely the anecdotal evidence of feeling and emotion that is now clearly happier, more confident, stronger, and more harmonious.

This sharing of information, logic, and evidence is in a way, a great example of how you can build confidence. You can in fact, build the confidence through the two departments of your brain, the conscious and subconscious. The same learning and developmental principles that are necessary in areas like mathematics and science, apply to the exercise and development of your mind. Just as performing scores of mathematical equations will increase your ability in solving equations, and your affinity for practicing them, so too will your habitual thoughts, that are impressed upon your subconscious mind, and your persistent behaviors increase your ability to overcome perceived obstacles that you face in your life.

A woman once told me about the fears that she had about the responsibility that she had incurred on the job. She stated that she was not able to sleep due to the mounting pressures from her boss and security department members. This woman worked in a jewelry department in a major department store and was responsible for showing the merchandise to customers, ringing up sales, and the overall security of the merchandise. She said that recently the security department had put in cameras due to high theft in her area and she was worried that the security personnel were going to set her up to make it look like she was stealing from the company. I told her that her fear was based on the perception of what they were doing and she needed to change her mindset. I explained to her about the Life Force that longs to be expressed through her in the form of confidence and right action.

I gave this woman a prayer that I asked her to pray on two times daily for a time until she saw a change in her perceptions. This prayer calls upon the Life Force for strength, guidance, and right action. It is as follows:

"God in me thinks, speaks, and responds to all things in my environment. God always wishes well for me as I am a medium through which he lets his love, strength and leadership flow. God always gives me enough of what I need, and he prepares the path I travel so I can be safe, happy, and well."

The Unfathomable Power Of Prayer

How does prayer work? Prayer works through faith which is one of man's quintessential stumbling blocks. The stumbling block for man is that, if it can't be proven in some method of science that is physical and tangible and able to be regularly repeated and quantified, it doesn't exist. Faith is a precious, fundamental piece of human kind with which no other animal or species has been blessed.

Prayer, when used properly, (there is no way to fail in prayer, but it can be used for the wrong reasons) is a blessing-module and a filler. The blessing is placed into the mind displacing negative thoughts. The displacement of the negative thoughts by the prayer, works to push all negative thoughts out. This process leaves the mind filled with only the good news and truth of God which serves to fuel and strengthen the Life Force that endures within you.

Observing and giving praise for the Life Force that rules the world, is a method to fortify self-confidence. Giving credibility and faith to this power keeps it real in your life and flowing from you as it inundates your every thought and behavior. Although this life force is invisible to man's eyes, it is extremely material to man's heart. The overwhelming feeling that supports you and builds your level of confidence, further proves to those who exercise the Life Force with their personal desires, that it exists. Take heart in this and you will be moved on a journey of life that only the faithful have the pleasure of experiencing.

There is no reason for anyone to continue living their lives in trepidation or the anticipation of bad happenings. God gives us his power and asks us to use it like a shield of armor that we carry with us at all times. If you get scared, turn to the shield with the words "God speaks, acts, and responds through me." With these words you can not fail, because in saying them and having faith in the almighty power, you have just called to him and asked him for help. Let the Divine Master of all the Ages take over for you and do that which you asked to be done through you.

If you're feeling substandard in the throes of a dilemma that has been formulated from your here-to-fore negative thoughts and beliefs, call on the power of God inside you to lead you to the course of right-action, on the path that he will make safe and comfortable for you. Don't waste any more time on your empty thoughts of inferiority. Don't try to lead yourself out of the situation. If you're in a situation that is that dire and hopeless and you are overwhelmed, then let go of the situation and let God take you forward to overcome the obstacle with his divine power, grace, humility, wonder, and might. Pray for guidance and right action when you need it, and believe that it will work for you, straightening all the bumps on your road of life.

For every difficult challenge you face, your faith will lead you through. Acquiesce your position to God, for he is there and will gladly help you through your troubles. Then, begin to surmount the situation and be victorious over all odds and difficulties. Take on the situation and the power of God will come to assist you in full force. You will be triumphant because you have the faith to let God solve all your problems and overcome your most difficult obstacles. Let the light of your life shine through you to the outside world, and God will be pleased that you let him act through you to show his absolute power and strength.

Time To Organize

It is just amazing to me when I see someone succeed or overcome, without understanding that their accomplishment was assisted by the divine powers of the Lord. It doesn't matter what religion you are or what sect you belong to, or what you call God, Jesus, Jahwe, Jehovah, Creator, Allah, or Buddha. The principles of all the major religions are correct. They all teach about the three things that God is, The Light, The Truth, and The Way. All successful people, no matter what religion they profess, rely on the powers of their God. They are aware of the Life Force, in some capacity, that leads them to success in everything they do.

Anyone can call on the creator of the Life Force at any time and gain satisfaction in the knowledge that if they believe, he will provide. He most certainly will provide, usually in greater abundance than you asked, because he wants to see you prosper and do well in his name.

Love One Another

All major religions and religious sects also teach that you should love one another. The reason for this is fairly obvious. As you are a living, breathing, and fully functional vessel for the Life Force of your God to use as a medium, you should respect yourself and others who possess the Life Force. He wants you to be consumed by the divine love that he has given you. It is to be used by you and shared with others through you. He wants his eternal, omnipotent powers of love, beauty, and wisdom to be free flowing through you to all people, for the love you show others helps to show off the Life Force and other eternal blessings that he has given.

Your Energies Are Amazing!

Every difficulty that you are faced with in life is able to be overcome with the supreme and unwavering powers that are stored up inside you to be brought out when you call upon them. The challenges that you are confronted with are no match for the powers of your divine energies. If God be for us, who can be against us? Let yourself become inspired to dream up new and innovative methods to overcome those obstacles that pop up on your journey. Live for challenges, because victory over them is used to showcase the incredible talents that are available to you.

Conserve and economize your energies. Take care in the consumption of your thoughts by assuring that they are invested wisely in good, just, and right ideals. Think about what will come, think about what will happen, and be sure that the occurrences that you think will happen are the favorable outcome. Don't waste your time or your thoughts, your talents or your gifts, on the negative possibilities, because the possibilities are just that—possibilities. You have to believe that every outcome will benefit you. You are what you think every moment of every day, so think wisely, think well, and think of yourself in the best possible terms.

The Formula For Life Success Through Prayer

You want to save the day? You would like to become an opera singer? You want to become an astronaut? No matter what it is that you want, there is a formula that will get you there. Let me show you the prayer formula. You have the Life Force alive inside of you (x). You have a desire that you would like to have fulfilled (y). You have a mind to think of what may or may not happen, and in that mind you have to have faith in the best possible outcome (z). You have the gift of providence that lives in you and mingles with your Life Force (a). {See Next Page}

	Life Force (x)
+	Desire (y)
+	Faith (z)
+	Providence (a)

Success in all that you want to achieve.
The power to accomplish all that you want.
The ability to overcome all obstacles.
The blessing to live a life of happiness and joy.
Beauty displayed when you walk into a room.

The Gift Of Truth

What is the one gift that you must have for all this to work? You must have belief that your God has placed this Life Force in you to assist you at every avenue of your life and to be there with you through thick and thin. The Life Force is provided. The free-will given to all people is what you need to bring to the classroom in your mind. You have to have a desire or a passion. You've got to have faith that this Life Force coupled with the desire will get you where you know deep down you want to be. The last necessity that has to be available to you, is the law of providence. This provides for those who need it, when they need it. It is always there, but you have to believe in it, not just a little, but fully believe in it and the capabilities of the law of providence.

All of the pieces of the equation are perfectly suited to work within the realm of the Life Force. These are pieces that you need to pick up along the way. No matter where you pick them up, when, or how doesn't matter. The only thing that matters is that you have them and you keep them available to yourself at every point in your life. These gifts can never be given, all people come upon them when the time is right and they are ready to accept them.

People usually find these gifts at the lowest point in their life. The gifts are there at every stage of life, but need to be seized, they need to be snatched up from the invisible barriers and obstacles that everyone places in front of themselves when they believe they have gone as far as they can. The moment these gifts are all pulled together, intertwined, and used together as a dominant force, is the moment you will benefit from their great individual and collective power. The moment you begin to use the power that these gifts have to offer is the moment you begin to make a difference in your life. The moment you feel that it is necessary to leverage a power far greater than that of the limitations of the human body and human mind, is the moment you will enjoy the great and unfailing support of these fine gifts from God.

Enjoy And Exercise Your Gifts

These amazing gifts can never be taken for granted, and will never fail you. These gifts will never be unavailable to you or have conditional use; they are unconditional. They are there, fully available and unconditionally assigned to you in all the days that you live. Just as your Life Force desires to be used so that your God can work through you to show the world the power, strength, and goodness that he has wrapped up inside all people, these other powerful gifts want to be exercised. These gifts are most powerful when used for good and to the benefit of others.

I am sure the people you know that are most successful, in your opinion, are people who do for others in unselfish ways that few can claim. These unselfish and successful people are an inspiration to all people and they function in that manner to display the incredible gifts that they have flowing inside their subconscious minds, through the power of the Life Force.

Greater Than The Riches Of The Fabled City Of Atlantis

These gifts can not be willed, yet they are as good as all the riches of Atlantis. These gifts can never be shared as everyone must acquire theirs on their own. The news of these gifts and how to reach them can be shared, that is what I am doing with this book. With the support and aid of these gifts you will never be hungry or thirsty, you will never be wanting or needy, you won't even be lonely and longing for someone's love. These gifts provide security and solace to all who possess and treasure them. In their proper use, they surely provide the salt to the earth.

These gifts have great power on their own, but for best results in desiring, and praying, (asking God to help you use them for what you desire) the gifts should be used jointly. You don't have to do anything special to maintain them, just exercise them whenever possible. You know the saying "use it or lose it." So whenever your desires well up inside you and you feel it is a good time to let loose the powerful gifts inside of you, just go ahead and do it, set them free and watch your life grow. Just be sure that your desire is what you want and need.

Alter Your Requests, Change It Up Occasionally

You will find that from time to time you will use this equation to reap the benefits and rewards that it avails you to, and you will receive nothing. At this point it might be best to try something else in your prayers to obtain the benefits that you seek. Try to mix up the words exchanging prayer vocabulary for everyday vocabulary, giving it more of a sense of an everyday request. Or perhaps you can ask for the benefit and call on your gifts at different times of the day. Or perhaps you could change the environment where you ask for the answer, solution, or gift. The equation for receiving the gift is correct, but every person is able to access the gifts in a slightly different manner, because of the different circumstances by which they assembled the power of their gifts.

Sometimes you will find that you get no results at all. This could be because your subconscious mind, where your Life Force dwells, is the model protector of your well-being. You may have your best interests in mind, and you may believe you are perfectly aware of what you want your desired benefits to be, but the Life Force has the added benefit of Boundless Knowledge. So in essence, the decision you make consciously may negatively affect your life, the Life Force instinctively has veto power so it can protect you. When this happens try to ask for your benefit in a different manner or at a different time. Perhaps a different place is what is needed. This will vary among all people. Keep your eyes open to small parts of the benefit that you seek. Sometimes it does not come all at once, but a piece at a time.

Boundless Knowledge knows all and sees all. You may not have consciously known or seen a serious negative consequence to a decision that you had purposefully made that will lead to your desired outcome, but your subconscious mind, having the powers of Boundless Knowledge, will recognize any dubious repercussions. You can not question it, because it is still not completely understood how this incredible intelligence is gained and from where the information is gathered.

Let Go, Let God

This incredible power of the subconscious mind and the powers contained within is proven daily when you try as hard as you can to find the answer to a question in your mind. Consciously you suffer to find the solution, then you give up. You don't think about it anymore. Before you know it, you have the answer. A miracle? Sort of, when you stop trying to consciously find the answer, this avails your subconscious to use more powers of your mind. This is when you will mysteriously attract the answer; it comes to you when you are not consciously focusing on it. You just have to turn it over to your God-given powers, because the answer is there. The Lord said ask, and it shall be given to you. Knock, and the door shall be opened unto you.

Your Desire Drives Your Outcome.

Part of faith is knowing that something that you desire is as real as the nose on your face. When your desire is this real and you know every aspect of every angle of every possible person that may look at the subject of your desire, then you are there. You know it is real even before it is. When this happens everything will undoubtedly come together, because when the subject of your desire is this real, the completion of the project, action, or support will have all necessary pieces for the development and completion.

I have studied people in person, in books, and through formal, structured interviews. I suspect you have done the same in many respects. I am quite certain that you have hired someone, or have been hired. It is in this process that you find out a lot about a person. I suspect also, that you have friends. Having friends that you are close to is an ongoing interview process. It is during these very informal interviews that you learn about your friends hobbies, likes, and dislikes and other peculiar behaviors and ideas that they have that help to grow a more enriching relationship.

Buy The House And The Ring

You have probably dated, or been engaged, or even married. In these processes the primary goal is togetherness and spending time to get to know each other better. It is to that end that the interview process is ongoing and ever-evolving. It starts with "how are you doing?" and goes all the way up to arrangements for the house after the kids move out. I find it so troubling however that people quite often have no plan for their life. I have heard a lot of "I'll see how it goes" responses, and that troubles me a bit, but I do know that whatever "I'll see..." means to these people, is available in definition in the hallowed halls of their subconscious mind and it is not my place to pry.

It is peculiar indeed, how people ever expect in the least, that they will forge ahead and be successful, when they are so noncommittal. How can you build a life of peace, happiness and abundance without any formal or informal plan of action for your life? Nobody in business will ever presume to start a business, run it, or proceed in it without a plan of action over a period of time. The time period is really rather irrelevant as the main point is that there is a plan at all.

What Does This Button Do?

The primary purpose that I ever ask questions at all is because it is not possible to organize the small working parts of your life, much less the big ones, without first posing an array of questions to your Life Force and Boundless Knowledge. It is those two pieces that are able to establish an effective answer in an organized manner that your subconscious mind can act on, in fulfilling the function of what you desire. Taking action is left to the powers of the Life Force and is driven by desire. Your Boundless Knowledge, knowing that you consciously want an answer to such a question, provides the answers for you so that your Life Force available inside your subconscious mind can begin to act on it. It's a beautiful and amazingly complex system in operation inside of you, but to work it, all you have to learn how to do is push the "on" button, which is desire.

Keep in mind that what a man thinks in his heart, during every moment of his life, he will become. This is true because you are what you think. So, if you are not currently where you want to be or who you want to be, then let your mind ponder perpetually on those things, and they will soon come. Set your mind free from the failures of the past and the boundaries that you previously set for yourself. Think instead, and dwell upon the limitless possibilities that lie ahead for you, because there are no boundaries, except those which you believe. Think about what you want to do and who you want to be. Desire this with all your heart and you will be all that you wish.

Would You Like To Be Healthy?

To think happy thoughts and apply happiness and joy to your life during your day is a large ingredient to living a happy and healthy life. That's right, because your physical health is largely controlled by the emotions that you experience. Your emotional stability is determined by the way you think all day long. Again, so much of who we are and what we do, what kind of health we have, and what kind of experiences we are able to have, is controlled by the thoughts that we convey within ourselves and reveal to the rest of society. Therefore, your physical health is directly brought about by your emotional wellness. The mind-body connection is once again a primary component in your well-being.

Some tips to provide better health for yourself are as simple as letting the little stressors and distractions in your life just pass you by without worry or grief. Refusing to worry about what you can't control, and doing your best on those things you can control, doing so in this manner will save you from needlessly looking back on them and worrying about the outcome. All you can ever do in your life is the best of what you have to offer in any situation. If your best is given, then you have to feel confident (have faith) that everything will turn out for the best.

Don't strain yourself emotionally about that which is out of your hands. The strain will only cause physiological symptoms to which you don't need to be subjected. These physiological symptoms are the way the Life Force tells people that don't perceive the subtle signs, that their negative thoughts are not the proper use of the faculties that were provided to them. The more that a person lets the signs go, without action to change the negative thoughts, the more troubles arise and are written on the physiology of the body.

If you tend to hold grudges, you must relinquish them. You need to let go of ill feelings towards other people. The Life Force of God is being suffocated by these feelings. God loves everyone and a grudge is an anger, or a hatred, which is likened to murder. The Life Force can not do good with all that negativity and hatred being fortified in the mind. You must release it, let it go, and focus on the positive things in your life and all the good people with which you associate.

The manifestation of negative feelings and thoughts is usually in the form of illness, lack of success, troubled thoughts beyond the grudge, and an inability to focus. What you need to remember is that outside forces have no impact on you and everything that happens to you is directly linked to your behaviors, thoughts, and actions. If you are prone to illness, bad luck, or worry, it can be changed by changing the thoughts in your mind.

You simply should never use your Life Force to wish harm or suffering on someone. That is the equivalent of taking a precious gift given to you by someone you respect, and using that gift to harm that person or their family. Everyone is a child of God and therefore loved by God. The gift of the Life Force should never be used in conjunction with a grudge or a hatred that you have for another human being. God gave you the power of the Life Force so you could go out and make a positive difference in the world by exerting your will through your desires. This is God's wish for the use of the Life Force inside you and he is always proud when it is used in this manner.

Produce Health And Well-being

And when he was come into the house, the blind men came to him-and Jesus said unto them, "Believe me that I am able to do this?" They said unto him, Yea, Lord. Then touched he their eyes, saying, "According to your faith be it unto you." And their eyes were opened...
Matthew 9:28-30

These words spoken by the savior of all people, presents the argument for faith, and the overwhelming power it contains inside of you. No more must really be said about the power, than the words written in the scriptures. Surely this is conclusive proof for those that have faith, of the eternal power that faith has provided throughout the ages of humanity. Faith and belief are strong, just how strong is a question that is answered every day by those who can tell amazing stories of personal triumph and consolation to anyone willing to listen.

It is your divine right to be healthy, so you should keep your conception of being well. Focus and emphasize your desire on getting well and staying well. Such feelings and emotions being showered out from you onto the world and your own subconscious mind will motivate the Life Force within to apply health and well-being onto you. Wellness and proper health will soon be yours.

In order to gain and maintain health, your thoughts have to be healthy and in the spirit of goodness and benevolence. I have talked to many people who were sick, who had never been sick in the past and lived very healthy lives up to that point. The doctors sometimes could explain what had caused the deterioration of good health and sometimes they could not. I talked with these people and found through the years that they all had one thing in common. These people, each one of them, was in the process of some very difficult times in their lives where a large change of thought and happiness had occurred. Some were in the process of divorce, some found out that a loved one was ill, some were unhappy in their jobs, and some were going through negotiations in preparation for a life change in a different way. All great challenges led to the deterioration of their physical health after the diminishing of their mental health.

All of these people, although they had different challenges and different paths to overcome their challenges, had the same basic thoughts cycling through their minds. All of these people were thinking terrible thoughts of other people that they believed to be key components of their struggles and life-changes. They were all worrying, resentful, and they had feelings of hatred and antagonism. These negative thoughts, and the emotions that were associated with them, were the wrong thoughts to have, because what your Life Force thrives on are thoughts that trigger the opposite end of your spectrum of emotions.

It was the combination of the emotions and feelings that these people harbored, and the negative thoughts that they had, that led them to the negative physical condition from which they were now suffering. What you think in your heart (head) is what you become, there is no way around it. These people each gave the outward appearance of one who was not bothered, but inside they were a powder keg of emotions ready to explode with the slightest provocation. This mountain of frustration has to be released. After it has been completely released, fill your mind with thoughts of pleasure and good, and focus on your desires. This will fill the space in your mind so there is no room for the negative thoughts and emotions that can sometimes penetrate and steal attention and focus from the accomplishment of your desires.

It is important to always bear in mind that just as you are the perfect creation and expression of God, so too are the people that you interact with on a daily basis. Everyone you see is the creation of your God. If you are to believe that God is always with you and there for you, you need to believe the same for them. If they anger you and get you all boiled up inside, pray to your God that they will see how they hurt you, but communicate and continue to show your love for them in your thoughts and actions.

It is a real difficult idea to propose that the subconscious mind, which houses the powers of your Life Force, is going to be able to provide a healing fortress within you, when that same house is occupied in wrongful thinking. If the prayers you pray are not effective, if the desire you choose is not being executed, then it may be time to rummage through the content of your thoughts and dispose of those thoughts and ideals which are not pure, or in fact, are full of hate. How can you think to heal yourself, when you are thinking to kill or cause harm to another human-being. You must change your mind to bring about true and long-lasting change.

Your God-given Gifts Will Guide You.

Therefore if any man be in Christ, he is a new creature—Old things are passed away; behold, all things are become new. 2 Corinthians: 5:17

Another concept addressed earlier that deserves another touch, is the belief that external powers and influences can affect you. Clearly, people let outside factors settle into their thoughts. These thoughts in turn, affect the emotions that are associated with those outside factors. When you do this, you admit and acknowledge that the outside world has an affect on your life and how you live it. Giving power to outside forces, thoughts, and influence is minimizing the power that you possess inside of you. When you do this you are casting away your faith in the healing power of the Life Force inside of you and diminishing your belief and faith in the gifts that your God has bestowed upon you.

Offer Up Your Illness To God

Overcoming illness is not difficult. You must not fear what the sickness can do to you. You must not believe, no matter what has happened to someone else, that the sickness can kill, corrupt, or reduce you in your physical, mental, and spiritual being. You are above whatever power society has placed on illness, and you have no fear of it. You must steadfastly affirm and mean it, that you have perfect wholeness in your mind, body, and spirit. The image that you present to yourself will shift into your subconscious mind where your Life Force can go about making it happen. Keep in mind, no matter how far away you move from your internal powers consciously, your subconscious is always available and working, so you need to impress upon your subconscious all good and benevolence, all wellness and health, and all success and prosperity.

To be well and stay well, throw yourself into every project that you take up physically, mentally, and spiritually. This will keep you fit as a fiddle and filled with an abundance of power and vigor. Keep the intensity of your desire for your wellness at a high priority in your life, this will keep you well, through all your life's endeavors. Keep the knowledge and faith that all ailments come and go, none are with you to stay. Remember forever that the things you think are what you become. Think well, and you will be well.

Be Careful!!

Things are not always what they may seem to you. We've all seen the pictures, where depending on your overall life outlook, you can see the smiling and beautiful young woman or the old ugly woman. Illusion and deception are used everyday, sometimes on purpose and sometimes not. Do you question the validity and truth of the plethora of information you receive everyday? If you don't, you may be setting yourself up to believe and perpetuate the thoughts contained in the information. You must always remember that the things you choose to believe make up who you are. When you believe enough of what others say and do, you may not create ideas on your own or even want to think for yourself.

You are bombarded with statements and reports and late-breaking news. Your day is littered with bits of information to which you attach significance to, and sometimes even emotion and feelings. Those thoughts that you accept are emotionally charged in some way to you and your beliefs. You must not forget that the pieces of information that you accept as true are emotionalized by you, and have an affect on your, physical, mental, and spiritual substance. Prevent bad information from entering into your subconscious mind and affecting your overall health and well-being by filtering it effectively.

The workings of the mind are very complicated and above explanation by human knowledge, yet it is very simple to understand and maintain. The subconscious mind, the epicenter of your world is a finely tuned, quality honed, instrument, that is a gift from above. All of our believed thoughts enter into it and are impressed upon it. From there we have an emotional tag that gets associated with it. From that point, anytime that thought is recalled, the emotional tag comes with it.

You need to dispose of your perceptions that are impressed upon your mind, that have a negative emotion tied to them. You need to let go of all negative emotions associated with thoughts and clear your mind of this clutter. These thoughts only serve to hold you back and limit your ability to come to rational decisions and pure thoughts. Unhealthy thoughts cause you to regress from the point of your personal epiphany relating to the discovery of the blessings that have been given to you.

The negative associations prove that you are a slave to the belief that things that take place outside of your thoughts and ideals have a power over you, and this is simply not true. To the extent that you tie emotion to every single thought, shows just how much power you assign to it, when you shouldn't assign any. So please, reduce your emotions to other's thoughts, ideals, actions, threats, violence, stupidity, and hatred. Take heart and solace in the fact that your world exists for you and is self sufficient to care for you and provide for you. Refuse to give power to anything except your own thoughts of goodness, benevolence, and purity. This will purify and fortify your world in your mind, body, and spirit.

Where You Are Is Where You Have Worked To Be

A huge misunderstanding to most people is that they still attribute their lot in life to causes and effects outside themselves. People want to place blame on all kinds of circumstances that they believe are wildly beyond their control. They try to lay criticism on outside conditions and circumstances that exist outside of the realm of their own mind. The truth is and has always been, should people finally notice, that all challenges are caused by psychic and intellectual patterns that are established in the mind.

Take heart that the things that happen around you in every corner of the world that are close or far away, do not have any ability to affect the world in which you live. The things that are out there are absolutely not the things that are causing you heartache, despair, pain, grief, agony, melancholy, or disrepute. They are only things and actions that paint the world it's color. It is how you mentally respond to these things, or choose to not respond to these things, that color your own world and cause you the difficulties and tribulations or happiness and triumphs in your life.

It's a shame that some people are stuck with the belief that their lot in life, in the way of their health, is determined by diet and genetics. In my wanderings, I have heard many people say that they have a disease because it is hereditary, or that they have weight difficulties because of heredity. This thinking is wrong. Every living person has the power of free-will. This free-will gives every person the right and privilege to accept or reject everything and anything that they hear or perceive. The blaming of their personal physical challenges on something beyond their control is ignorant, because the truth is that they control everything. There is nothing that anybody says or does that can affect your health in any way unless you let them affect your health.

Are You Looking Out For #1?

Doctors are good and have done miraculous work in the field of medicine to help people overcome challenges in their lives. This is great!! Medical and pharmaceutical researchers have done plenty to advance pain relief, healing, and recovery. Researchers have your best interests in mind some of the time, but the truth is, their primary interest is in the benefits that they can bring to their companies in the form of revenue. There have been many miracle drugs approved by the FDA that have later been proven to have terrible side-effects that render people worse off than before they began the so-called miracle treatment. Researchers do have your best interest in mind, some of the time, but you have your best interests in mind all of the time, because to you, you are #1.

Why not look out for #1? Why not tell yourself today and forever that you know what is best for you, you know what you want, and you will do whatever is in your natural God-given powers to take full control of all the decisions in your life. Tell the Doctors and the Researchers that you are fully aware of the natural healing powers in the body and you intend to use them to overcome the physical and mental obstacles that have crept onto your path, and make yourself better. Take Control! The Subconscious Mind and all the powers contained within, work on the basis of laws. The laws of your mind are much stronger than the written laws of man that envelope you in the day-to-day activities of your life.

Because the subconscious mind is based on the set of laws that control your world, it works on a complex system of organization. The subconscious mind deposits all of your conscious and subconscious thoughts, into files that it stores, in order of importance, to be referred to, when you need them at a later date. The negative thoughts that are stored in your subconscious mind are the causes of all your ills. The positive thoughts that are stored in your subconscious mind are the wonderful makers of all of your life achievements and victories.

Here is a prayer I have used in the past to quell the negative thoughts that I have had throughout my life. The negative thoughts which have been deposited on my subconscious mind, in effect reducing the positive flow of the Life Force which was to be used in the manner for which it was designed, goes a little something like this:

"Let the Glory and Splendor of God's Light shine in my mind and offset the damaging effects of the negatives that I have knowingly or unknowingly imprinted on my subconscious mind."

This will take effect and take hold of your belief system and rip out all the evil and wrong thoughts that peek through and cause you failure and pain. You must be patient, faithful and believe in your powers that are given to you by the hand of your God.

You Control Your Health 100%

Many people that I have spoken to have stated adamantly that they have friends and relatives that are sick and are not able to recover with the help of a doctor and that these folks are sure to die, or live lives of discomfort. They ask me why God would do this to them when they are such good people. Clearly they misunderstand the power and scope of the mind. What they believe is that the sickness has nothing to do with anything that they could take power over. They believe that what has afflicted them is something that they can not control, something that just happened to infiltrate their lives and render them sick. This can not be the case, because everyone controls their physical, mental, and spiritual well-being through the powers of healing and wellness contained in their mind. The condition of all of these entities is affected only by the thoughts that you place and keep in your mind.

Thinking that you don't control your well-being spiritually, mentally, and physically, is a terribly wrong train of thought that offers you up to the happenings of the outside world. Nothing could be further from the truth. Every aspect of your life is in your control, therefore health and sickness is in your control. The control comes in the form of thoughts and ideals that you plant in your mind and how much control you allow the outside world to demonstrate over you. Sickness is dependent on the mind and has everything to do with the way you think and what you think. This is just one more example of how you are what you think all day long. Always think good thoughts. Employ courageous and enlightened ideals that foster benefits for you and others who live in your world.

There aren't any conditions that are unchangeable and there are no diseases that are incurable. There are however people in the world that have views, thoughts, and ideals which are unfruitful and sometimes destructive, making their overall lives incurable and devoid of all remnants of their God-given power. All these people will have to do is realize that nothing has power over them, not sickness, not people, and not any action that is at work outside of their minds. The only power that anything or anybody has, is that power which is given to it in your thoughts. If you believe it's true, then it is true.

All of us have countless beliefs that we have harbored since our childhood, they've been hidden away in the nooks and crannies of our subconscious mind. We never think about them or exercise them, but they are there. These beliefs that we have that we never use are nonetheless still with us, this being true, they still have the power to manifest themselves in our lives. This manifestation of long forgotten beliefs, be it good or bad, still have all the power of our Life Force to transform and inspire our lives. This is why it is good to find the positives of life and change your views, ideals, and beliefs along these lines. Always keep the positive and healthy thoughts in the forefront of your subconscious, so your Life Force can work on inspiring your life accordingly.

Each day you should aspire to extinguish the negatives from your subconscious mind. Begin each day with prayer, read the Psalms and reassure yourself of the great powers that God has given you in the form and function of your subconscious mind. Exercise your Life Force daily and create a routine whereby the Life Force starts to change the way you think and act. Let the Life Force that is within you, that is a gift from God, do your speaking, thinking, and acting. Create your life first in the subconscious mind through these exercises, then the subconscious mind and the Life Force contained within will use these thoughts to formulate your life in the fashion you desire.

There are many people who place the onus of their life's conditions and environment on external factors. As you now know, these factors have no control or bearing on your life due to the power that each individual has to choose their own life, and desire what they are to become. The environment around you, the people around you, and the thoughts that exist around you, are all there because of the choices that you have made in your life You have had ideas of who you want to become, or in some cases who you think you need to become, or in other cases still, who you think you have no choice but to become. This is a false belief and not the kind of thinking that you should be doing in creating your life in the fashion you desire. Fashion yourself in a design that you choose, and be happy and joyous in the development of your new and fully realized you.

Keep your thinking process clear and focused. Keep your ideals pure and dignified. Keep your dreams set on the stars above, so that you may choose to rise to a point in your life where you are exceedingly happy with the person you have become. Never let go of your necessary right to filter out and repel negative thoughts and influences on your life. Never let anyone or anything guide you, because you know what you want for you, and from you, and you are the best navigator on the road that leads to the accomplishment of your desires. Always exercise your Life Force in a positive manner, so that you can commit to all of the good that your ideals lead you to and cancel out all of the negatives that constantly bombard your thinking.

When you continually repel and routinely terminate negative thoughts and images in your subconscious mind, you are able to strengthen your Life Force. The more you perform these acts, the less often the negatives will persist to invade and thrive in your mind. Keep feeding your mind the good and the positive and leave no room for the negative, as it will use the Life Force to try to bring ruin to you, through constant worry and incessant fear. The negative thoughts come around less often where they know they are not welcome. Place a "Beware of Dog" sign on all the doors that lead to your mind and repel the negative thoughts that try to infiltrate your mind and terminate the positive thoughts that are flowing through it. Use this prayer to expel the negatives and increase the positive power of the Life Force within:

"Let the Glory and Splendor of God's Light shine in my mind and counter the damaging effects of the negatives that I have knowingly or unknowingly imprinted on my subconscious mind. Fortify my Life Force with the power of positive thinking and increased determination to build all aspects of my subconscious mind. Provide me with the building blocks of ideals, dreams and desires which will do well for myself and others. Let God's Infinite Wisdom fill my soul and offer up reasoning to temper and terminate the existence of all negative thoughts."

The only truth that matters when working with the Life Force contained in your subconscious mind is that nothing and nobody can control your success, happiness, or health. Nobody can make you feel sad unless you emotionalize their actions in a manner that causes yourself to feel sadness, the same is true for depression and anger. Feelings are brought out from within you based on the experiences that you have had in your life and how you emotionalize each experience. All of these feelings and emotions are stored in your gigantic control box, your subconscious mind.

To build your courage and your innate ability within to overcome the obstacles that you will surely feel when commencing on trusting in yourself and believing only the positive truths from others, I have assembled a small list of Bible passages to lead you forward with courage and might. Enjoy them and gather strength through them.

He giveth power to the faint; and to them that have no might he increaseth strength.
Isaiah 40:29

Be of good courage, and he shall strengthen your heart, all ye that hope in the Lord.
Psalm 31:24

I can do all things through Christ which strengtheneth me.
Philippians 4:13

Acquire All Your Heart Desires

Changing your mind from rather negative to endlessly positive is not an easy task, but sometimes you have to perform some difficult tasks in order to attain those things you want. You have to understand that the person inside of you is the blessing from above, your body is just the vessel through which the powers inside you travel around this world. It is not about the things you wear, the way you look, or the house you live in, your beauty and potential comes from inside and everyone who looks, will see it. The things you have are benefits of the use of your internal powers.

You need to develop your internal powers to work for you by feeding them the good stuff of the world, instead of just existing while feeding all sorts of meaningless, and sometimes negative, thoughts and information into your mind. Be selective and put your mind on a diet, no more junk information, no more junk rumors and gossip, no more junk negative thoughts leading to negative emotions. Keep your mind focused and trained on your goals, so you are always in a place you want to be.

Right now it is easier living your life in the manner you live it, whether you're happy with it or not. You have the people around you that make you feel comfortable and you have a comfort zone in your job, but you just don't seem to be accomplishing those things that you thought you would like to do. Soon you will realize just how unhappy you are with it, you will desire more, have a complete change of mind, and begin to notice the substantial differences in your life that just a few changes of thought will make. When this happens, roll with it. Get on board the train of desire and ride it out of your unfulfilled life. You have to gather the ability and the strength to make changes in your life that will take you on your way to all that you desire.

Change your mind to change your life. You must decide to give up the marginal happiness that you have with the people, places, and things around you. It is time to put faith in the powers you possess internally to create a bold and new future. It's time to put faith in your possibilities and in the wisdom that you have collected in living the life that you have now. You need to put them all together and begin to reinvent yourself as the person you see in your dreams. The person you want to become is very near to you, you just have to reach out with faith in the amazing powers that God gave you, so you can acquire the life you really want.

Do you want to be a beauty queen, but have a bad complexion? Do you want to be a star actor or singer, but are scared of the public? Do you wish to be a major league pitcher, but falter in the middle innings? How about becoming a ballerina with weak ankles? Do you wish to be a construction contractor, but feel afraid to go off on your own? Or how about, you wish to be the head of the company that you work for, but nobody takes you seriously and you keep getting passed up for promotions? These situations, although all demoralizing and difficult to accept, are the kinds of challenges that people have hypnotized themselves to be afraid of for generations.

Have you ever stopped yourself from doing something because of the fear of failure, or are you right now wishing that you could overcome that perceived weakness that holds you down from that next rung of success? I wrote perceived and I mean perceived, but I do understand that perception is reality, therefore what you perceive is as real as the nose on your face or the thumb on your hand. Overcome negative perceptions and start to view the world as you want to. Make it a place where you can be all you want to be, take chances, throw yourself into the mix of the world by having faith in yourself and your internal gifts, and you will be successful.

Everybody in this world is special and everybody has a place. I hope that this truth is self-evident to you, although what is usually not self-evident is where that place is, and that differs from person to person, personality to personality, and place to place. You are necessary in this universe and wanted, but the trouble is sometimes discovering your need and aligning it with your want in a way that makes you comfortable. In order to find that place for yourself which will provide for you the riches of life that you seek, I have put together a couple of Bible verses for which to meditate and focus.

Riches and honour are with me; yea, durable riches and righteousness. My fruit is better than gold, yea, than fine gold; and my revenue that choice silver. I lead in the way of righteousness, in the midst of the paths of judgment: That I may cause those that love me to inherit substance; and I will fill their treasures. The Lord possessed me in the beginning of his way, before his works of old. I was set up from everlasting, from the beginning, or ever the earth was.
Proverbs 8:18-23

Wealth and riches shall be in his house: and his righteousness endureth forever.
Proverbs 112:3

Prayer Works!

In calling on your Boundless Knowledge that resides inside all the power of your subconscious mind, you are calling to your God in prayer. The truth is that everything you think is prayer to God. Let your thoughts praise him and rejoice in the victory that he has won for us by using your powers of the Life Force to work through you. In this process you are serving God and you will benefit from service.

The prayer is the ultimate gift to and from your God. This powerful gift serves dual purpose to all people who believe. The first purpose is to communicate with your Lord to ask him for the gifts that you would like to receive. The second purpose is two-fold. It is to show your Lord that you are a vessel through which he can work with his almighty power to accomplish his will, and to praise him for the phenomenal accomplishments with which he has blessed you.

A competent prayer session is effective when it is based upon the spiritual premise that your God, does indeed, work within you and through you. Competent prayer sessions also are performed with complete conviction, which results in the success of the prayers. Your prayers are usually in the form of personal desires which you would love to see come to fruition because it will enhance your life, or the lives of your loved ones in some way. Once the Life Force accepts the personal desire, it immediately works to make your desire come to realization.

Competent prayer is accomplished through having a clear and fully developed desire that you present to your subconscious mind. Competent prayer requires practice and conviction; it requires belief and a positive mental frame of mind by which you believe that the Life Force that you possess goes to work immediately making the necessary changes to bring about your desires. You must be very focused to impress upon the Life Force that your desire is real, and its accomplishment is in the works. Your Life Force will not fail to provide anything that you desire. Your Life Force reigns within you for this very purpose, because all the thoughts and desires that you possess are there for a reason.

With competent prayer you are essentially changing your mind to conform to the eternal truths of God. You won't ever need to beg for the completion of your desires. You will need to reorganize your mind, and desire the just rewards of life. A prayer that has been exceedingly successful for those who have prayed on it goes like this:

"I know there is a perfect law of distribution. I am always in touch with all things that I require in this world. I am guided to do those things which I am suited to do, and I am loving this marvelous process of life. I am giving of my talents everyday in every way and I am taking possession of a wonderful wage, consistent with my honesty and integrity in my life's pursuits."

This prayer when prayed two times a day, will offer a change from that life which you were living in the past, where all of the truths identified in this prayer were not always the truth. If you fail to see results immediately, or within fifteen days time, change the wording to more closely resemble your vocabulary. You will see dramatic rewards when this prayer is put to use in helping you to fulfill all of your life's desires.

Like a child who knows how to get his way, you need to be relentless in your pursuit of your desires through prayer. The thought and conviction that you commit to your desires in your subconscious mind, are like the light and water that a seed needs to grow. Keep up the pace, be persistent, ask, and ask, and ask again for what you want. Through God all things are possible, so don't just ask for enough to get by, ask for what you want to have and don't hold back. Keep on asking until you receive the response for that which you are hopeful. Be intense and certain that your desired outcome will appear for you, to satisfy you completely.

The great truths and power of your God are available to everyone, whether they be the world's most notorious criminal or the most successful and honest businessman. The Life Force flows in everybody making a notorious criminal able to use the infinite powers of the Life Force in the same manner as a Pastor or a Shaman would. The powers are not prejudiced or selective, they are not discriminate in any manner. Everybody has a true calling which they can aspire to, with the Life Force that is present and shining through them. Free-will allows all men to use the powers of the Life Force in the fashion that they choose.

If you are prepared now to buy into the invisible, yet very real powers of your God, which he has given to you and protected like a treasure inside your subconscious mind, then you are ready to reap the rewards of the many gifts that he has bestowed upon you in the form of talents. Believe wholeheartedly in the amazing powers that your God has given you. Understand the incredible achievements that you can have when you begin to utilize the relationship that you have with God, and cultivate your relationship through prayer. All power and might is available to you through your God, so if God be with you, who can be against you? Believe this and have your internal God-given powers shine like the light of a beacon, to all those who meet you.

Begin to refuse all other powers that you perceive could benefit or harm you. Nobody and nothing can cause you benefit or harm except that which you believe in your mind, so keep thinking pure thoughts and don't let negative outside influences affect you in any way. Be sure to filter all the messages from people, and all your perceptions of the world around you, so that you can have positive thoughts and emotions about all people, occurrences, and things in your life.

I have identified the four steps of successful prayer. Use these four steps in every prayer that you think and say and you will have satisfaction in all you desire. Here are the four steps to receiving all of your dreams and desires through prayer:

1) You have to acknowledge that your Lord will take care of you. He will provide for all your wants and needs. He will give you perfect health and all the success that you ask for. He will bless you with perfect relationships and family ties and invigorate your spirit to want more. He does all this when you acknowledge the law of providence in your mind. Your God created you, that was the tough part. Providing for you after he has done all the rest is effortless for him, and he loves to perform these services for you.

2) End giving power to anything outside of you and your mind that houses all of your God-given power.

It's easy to remember, after you start praying effectively and seeing the rewards given for the prayers, that there is nothing beneficial for you about giving power to anything or anybody outside of your Life Force, which is firmly established in your mind.

3) Declare with conviction that whatever difficulty enters into your world is met head on with the power of God inside of you. If God be for you, who can be against you. The mightiest armies and beasts have fallen to the power of God. No matter what religion you commit to, there are stories to show the immense power of your God who has, through the Life Force of one, or many, performed feats that astonish and amaze.

4) The fourth step is the easiest, yet the most forgotten. I enjoy this step immensely as it affords me many opportunities to pray. This step is, thank the Lord of your life for what he has given you. I sometimes thank him in advance, as I always know that what I ask for will come to me, oftentimes in greater riches than I had desired. Always take the time to pray. I offer the fourth step as a courtesy for all the Lord has given. Some people that I have given this advice to have committed to thanking the Lord, and some haven't, but I always believe that God is even more helpful when he knows that you credit him for the accomplishments that he brought about in your favor.

Please remember, the prayer doesn't have to be gaudy or wordy in any way. It is only meant to state in word and thought the many thanks that you have for what was given to you. A typical Thank You prayer goes something like this:

"Thank you Lord for the great gifts that you have given me. I shower praise and thanksgiving onto you for your incredible blessings which have always been present in my life, and the blessings that will continue to pave my path with the gold and riches of good fortune, health, success, happiness, and wealth."

This is a pretty simple prayer. The most important point to remember is that you want to give thanks for the newest, most current blessing as well as a blanket thanks that covers all of the many blessings of your life. I am sure if you were to sit down with a piece of paper and a pencil right now and begin to list all of your blessings on that sheet of paper, you would run out of room. Sometimes the many blessings that have been given to us are leading us up to the point where our dreams will be fulfilled without us even knowing that we were working in that direction.

Is The End, The End?

For this God is our God forever and ever: He will be our guide even unto death.
Psalm 48:18

There is no death in the form of nonexistence, only a death from the old and a rebirth into the new. As God lives in us now as that enduring Life Force, he will continue to dwell in us in whatever shape, form or fashion we take. God has no beginning and no ending, he is the Alpha and the Omega. He has always been there living in the hearts of those that love him. When this world passes away and our vessels have no longer the strength to endure, our body will decompose into the earth. Long before decomposition the Life Force inside will be lifted up and exalted for the accomplishments it has made in the name of our God.

The great gift that comes with death is that the Life Force or spirit that lives triumphantly through you will get to shed its vessel and move along life's path in a different form. You can't look at death as losing, be it in the form of a friend or a relative, only as a new beginning and a gain in the overall quality of their life. Certainly the Life Force takes a break for a time in order to meet up with long-past friends and relatives in a reunion of sorts, where it is able to take in all of the fruits of the labors on the earthly plane, and enjoy some time in solace where a soul can call home.

In this new place that is so good that it is referred to by many religions as a promised land or home place, the real wonders of your life, mind, and existence are shared with you. This is where you get all the information about what you were fully capable of on the earthly plane. It is where you will fully realize all of the monumental power that had been wrapped up inside you for so many years on the earth. It is where you will fully and clearly see everything that had transpired in your lifetime, how you reacted to it, and what difference you made in the overall picture. The place is so beautiful that you will believe the sun is shining on you every moment of every day and time passes slowly, so you can relax and enjoy it.

The life after this life is so good that ancient religions would have a wondrous series of ceremonies introducing the body into it's final rite of passage. This rite of passage has been hailed as the most glorious and extraordinary of all. It is a look back at the previous life and a celebration of the life to come. As a human being your life is endless, both in possibility and purpose. There is nothing on this earth that is comparable to the renewal that is brought on by death.

Death is more than an end to you or any of your family members and friends. It is as glorious as ancient religions make it out to be. It is a time where you will fully know all of your spiritual and mental capacities. You will recognize all people and be recognized by all people. You will be adored for all of your accomplishments and applauded for all your sacrifices. The greatest riches that you will ever see will be bestowed upon you, and all of them just for joining your friends in the next stage of life. The earth provides the proving grounds while the heavens provide the feast and celebration.

This end will be a new beginning for you in which you will understand the freedoms that are available to you. The endless expanse of creativity will open up to you where you can paint the picture for the rest of your life, and it will be more rewarding than this life. This much truth is certain. This much truth is fact, and this much will be yours to hold dear until your passage to the next realm. Someday friends will mourn and friends will rejoice. The earthly plane friends will yearn for your company and be sunk down in heavy hearts, if they don't understand the greatness and splendor of the advancement of your life. The heavenly plane friends will rejoice for eternity for the honor of your presence. You are a good person so the rejoicing will never end.

For God so loved the world, that he gave his only begotten son, that whosoever believeth in him should not perish, but have everlasting life.
John 3:16

As all men realize they are immortal, this passage becomes more and more certain, and even more meaningful. Death is just a stage. A very short stage in the process of existence that transfers the powers and energies of this lifetime into the next. In the next lifetime, perhaps a different shape will be taken, but all of the meaning that you have harvested from this world will be with you. With the power of

Boundless Knowledge at your disposal in the deeper workings of your subconscious mind, you will take an unlimited measure of knowledge with you. All you have to do to accumulate this knowledge for your next lifetime is, realize and utilize the immense powers at work in your subconscious mind.

Life is an endlessly evolving development. It continues to develop and realize well after the human form is buried in the ground or spread out across the countryside. Those who believe that life is finite and death is definite, don't really understand how this Life Force available and working inside of all humans works. God has given you the Life Force in the form of spirit available in the complex workings of your subconscious mind so that you never have to die. You will continue on my friend, forever and ever. God gave his son so this could be true.

It has always been imperative to the well-being of those who grieve, to turn their emotions around and rejoice for the better life of the friend or relative who has departed from this world. This is not such an easy thing to do, especially for those who believe that life is finite, or that death ends everything. The rejoicing is not for their own feelings of loss, but instead, the rejoicing is for the new found freedom from earthly bonds that our earthly body places on the full dynamics of our Life Force. When someone dies, they get the prize. They get to see what life is there for them to begin living in full spirit without the restrictions that the earthly body has imposed.

Friends and relatives who love the departed, will always feel a loss, because they miss having that friend to be close to, to laugh with, and to confide in. They can temper these feelings through prayer. They can pray that their friend has a wonderfully smooth transition to the heavenly plane, they can pray that they meet up quickly with the loved ones they had lost. They can pray for the departed to enjoy and marvel in the newfound treasures that their life has led them to, and they can pray for the accomplishment of new goals that they will set in the new life for themselves.

Having read many books on dying and death and having had death around me with family and friends, I had grown to understand early that those who pass away generally have no fear of what is to come, and oftentimes say that they know what to expect in the next life and look forward to the experience immensely. When I first realized that this was the general opinion and demeanor of those dying, I was in shock. I was very young and mostly ignorant to what lay ahead. As I have grown in spirit and in Life Force and have grown in the ways of life and death, illness, poverty, and so on, I have been able to pull together many pebbles of knowledge and wisdom. I have pieced them together into an overwhelming knowledge and comfort of the life and death conditions that we as humans, experience.

If I can impress upon you just one shred of knowledge from this book and you get nothing else from it, I would like to have you know that the peace and tranquility of the dying and the dead is the single greatest peace and comfort that any human can experience on the road of life.

Life has no beginning and no end. You will always live your life, in God and through God, just as he lives his life in and through you. Enjoy the time with your loved ones and develop relationships, because they are sure to continue in the heavenly plane. You surely should not cry or mourn for your loved ones as they will always be with you in spirit, and someday again physically. We will move from this earthly plane in peace and pick up right where we left off in the heavenly plane, in perfect peace and tranquility. Enjoy your life now, and you will really enjoy it at the day of your natural human progression.

Recovery From Illness

People always talk about how they have such illnesses and pain. I have been asked by people with all sorts of physical ailments, why does it happen and how can I rid myself of it? I am not a doctor of medicine nor do I want to become one, but I do have words of wisdom that when acted on, produce miraculous results. The results are truly amazing to most people, because they don't understand the healing powers of the mind and just what they are capable of each and every time you call upon those powers to heal. From swollen hands and skin conditions to troubles with backaches and sleep disorders, I have heard it all and have advised in the following manner.

Free your mind of all resentful, hateful, and vindictive thoughts towards other people. Purge your mind of all impure thoughts and the disdain that you carry with you for other people. Your body is a temple and your mind is the altar. You need to offer pure and good thoughts to your mind in order for your mind to have an antiseptic environment in which to work and carry out the requests and desires of health and well-being. You must drop grudges and desire to rectify the situation with whomever you feel spite, anger, bitterness, or the extreme--hate.

Let go of your own mistakes and wrong-doings. Everyone makes mistakes and everyone offends others occasionally--this is part of living. We all have emotions that are married with our past experiences, and those emotions are enhanced when an unpleasant experience happens again. Oftentimes we feel regret and disgust for the way that we react to a situation. People must learn to live in the moment and prepare for those moments, make it a point to react differently and emotionalize differently the next time a similar experience comes about. This will save you from feelings of shame and guilt, and free up your mind for the good things that you are able to accomplish.

You have to accept responsibility for your actions. Most of all, you need to forgive yourself for your mistakes in your previous experiences and make amends for any wrong-doing that you have caused to others. This will free you up to start living your life again without the fear of any more guilt or shame. Making amends will also return benefits and rewards to you in kind, as recompense for your generosity and forgiveness. A prayer that I ask those who suffer, to pray upon goes like this:

"The Life Force that heals, knows all the functions and capacities of my human body. This Life Force flows through me now rendering all of my capacities of mind, body, and spirit splendidly capable in every way. I feel inspired by the presence of the glory of God and I desire to act in a way that gladdens him. I forgive everyone through the power of his holy name and I furnish love and the blessings from the Lord upon all who I have wronged in my lifetime. Surely good things will come to those for whom I pray."

The benefits that you will see in the form of peace of mind will be all that you can handle. One time, a man I know, said that the benefits in his life from the dispensing of vengefulness and hate had transformed his life. He said that doing this had made a forty-five year old man feel like he had new life in the skin of an eighteen year old, fresh out of high school. The whole world looked different and seemed to hold unending promise and treasures. All chronic aches and pains that he attributed to every condition known to man had disappeared. Currently he is living a vibrant and energetic life of enjoyment and happiness.

Overcoming Life's Obstacles

I really want to be successful, but I can't seem to claim success in what I do.

Everybody says they want success, but most of the time I find that the success that people want is not clearly defined, or the desire to truly be successful is not present. You need to truly desire this success in whatever area of your life you call for it. You can do this by knowing that it will take place. Have a clear picture of what that success looks like to you, what you will be doing, how you will be acting, what you're wearing, what kind of house you're living in and what people you have surrounded yourself with in the process of getting there. Be as clear and definite as possible, really focus to see yourself living your life successfully.

The formula for the creation of this desired dream is like this:

Life Force + Desire + Faith +Providence = Success in all that you want

In this case you want success. You have the Life Force idly waiting for you to call upon it. You must now develop the desire. Come up with reasons why you want to have success, a better life, recognition, and prestige. Have reasons why you want to be liked and well-respected, or simply why you want to have the riches of the earth that success oftentimes brings.

Faith is a necessity in the accomplishment of an objective. You have to have faith that you will accomplish your objective. Faith will keep you strong until you achieve your desired outcome, and will keep you thinking in a positive manner to keep your Life Force focused on the completion of your objective. Without faith there is not a way in the world that your objective could be completed, because not having faith or belief in what you want to accomplish, gives you no reason to try.

Providence is what stirs in your omnipresent Life Force. Divine Guidance is the inspiration to the Life Force and it is what in particular gives you your strength and your edge, your will and your confidence. With this gift of God, ever-present, stirring in your Life Force, you will be taken on a life adventure that never bores you, never fails you, and always keeps you looking out for your next challenge.

If you want success you must become convinced that success is yours to be had. You must insist that the Life Force that swells inside your subconscious mind, takes you to where you desire to be. Your God created you in his image, so why would he not want you to have everything you want? You can be sure that there is no reason, so desire to have all the things in life you choose, and he will make it so.

If you want success, you must conclude giving power to external forces in your life. You must stop thinking of excuses of why you can or can't, other than excuses that are directly related to you, and controlled by you. Nothing is for chance, if you want it so, then it is so. There is nothing and nobody that has any control over you or the environment in which you operate. Excuses are for the unfaithful and the unclean of mind, you must know better than to blame someone else, no matter what the situation or consequences that happen in your life. You are the master of your universe and nobody can impact your universe without your approval.

You must know that if God be for you, nobody can be against you. If they choose to go up against you, they will surely lose. The immense power of God is read about in the Bible, is storied through story keepers, and is evidenced in the beauty of our world and the intricate workings of your mind. Don't lose hope. Keep strong, though the tide of tribulation is high.

Give thanks to the Lord your God for the gifts of completion and realization of all your desires. This is a necessary step in the continual growth of your abilities, to focus and demonstrate the God-given powers of your subconscious mind. Here is a prayer that puts it all together for you:

"The Life Force that joyfully dances a beautiful dance in my subconscious mind is hearing my every thought and prayer and is alive and present in me always. God's ideas are one with mine and my desire is to become successful in ______________________________. I know that God's gifts are available to me in unending bounty and I will see them perform with unbelievable skill and might in assisting me to accomplish my desires. Heavenly guidance will provide for me all that I need and make available an abundance of divine thoughts so that I may stimulate my Life Force to furnish all my desires."

In short, the only parts of this always-effective equation that you have to worry about are the desire to achieve and the belief that the achievement will transpire. Life Force and Providence are ready and waiting for you to tap into them. Now that you know how, through prayer and good thoughts, you can not fail to be successful, go out into the world and be the salt of the earth.

I Want To Get Well And Be Healed Of My Sickness

The equation never changes, it is as follows:

Life Force + Desire + Faith + Providence = Success

The Life Force is always there for you, although it may be dormant from nonuse. Create desire, visualize that which you want to happen. If you are constantly sick, see yourself being the vibrant, energetic person you used to be, all over again. You once were well, so your Life Force knows how to make you well again. Keep visualizing the great life that you will lead with your perfect health. Make the desire big and make it everything you want it to be.

Have faith in the outcome, do not sit around waiting to make plans until it happens. Start planning your new life, filled with all of the fun and excitement that you used to have. Think well and be well. Be strong in the faith that God has provided you with all the gifts you need to make yourself better. You know people make themselves well everyday, so why should you be different. Before today, the difference was that they believed and you didn't. Today there is no difference between you and somebody who has recovered, you are well on your way!

Providence (Divine Intervention) is already here for you. It is the stuff that led you to the purchase of this book. It is what has been stirring inside you since you decided that you wanted to be well. Providence is the trump card, that you will never play without. When you look for help, reassurance, and guidance, feel strong because providence is ready to assist you. Everyday in every way, providence strives to get you where you want to be.

The four steps to receiving all of your dreams and desires through prayer are conviction in the success of your desire's completion, negation of the thinking that anything outside of you has power over you, belief of the God-given power inside you, and praise to the Lord for making everything right. These four points will never change and are the defining pillars of the prayers you create to assure the achievement of your desires.

Here is a prayer that puts it all together for you:

"The Life Force that heals, knows all the functions and capacities of my human body. This Life Force flows through me now, rendering all of my capacities of mind, body, and spirit splendidly capable in every way. All the organs of my body understand the powerful and direct effects that are created through the presence of the Life Force and it's healing powers, and are responding now. Every whit of my being is being transformed and returned to perfection by the healing power. I surrender now to the perfect healing power that is reconstructing me and I give thanks for this magnificent gift."

A Foolproof Practice To Strengthen Self Confidence

Once again, here is the equation that never fails and never changes:

Life Force + Desire + Faith + Providence = Success

Two times per day, meditate and focus on this prayer. Give the Life Force the attention that it deserves through your prayers to God. Be sure that your thoughts are clean and pure when you enter into your prayer. When you start noticing a difference in your life or the way that you act and interact, please further remember to pray, praise, and give thanksgiving for your miraculous transformation that is only possible through the unending power of your Holy Father.

"Heavenly Love shines down upon my path to make it wider. The Lord's hand touches my heart to increase the size of my shoulders and the thickness of my skin. The powerful and far-reaching effects of the Lord upon the earth makes people delight to be in my presence and long for my words. The Infinite Wisdom which rests in the home of my subconscious mind bestows upon me, right action. God's power within me speaks, acts, and responds to all things to make my messages clear and full of vigor and genius. I give thanks for the wonderment of God that he has donated to me, to overcome the weaknesses that my mind used to dwell upon. I will prosper in all ways."

Never lose sight of the fact that you have to provide in every detail, the desire and belief, to make the equation that leads to success possible. This does require a little thought, because your Life Force does not know how you want it to act, or in what direction to take you, without it.

How Can I Change My Whole Life?

A whole life change probably isn't the answer. You are on the path to doing something in your life for which you are destined to do, but you may have taken a couple wrong turns in some areas of your overall life. If you feel that your whole life is wrong and you need assistance figuring out even the small details of the benefits that you have going for you, you may need to spend some time with a counselor, a pastor, a priest, a doctor, a teacher, a hypnotherapist, a psychiatrist, a relative, or a friend that can help you to sort through the very confused thoughts in your mind.

I can't recall a time where I talked with someone, and a decision was made to start from scratch and revamp their entire life. The mind doesn't work like that, it may be suffocated by your inability to bring the wonderful powers to bear, but the mind somehow finds a way to keep you reasonably close to the answers you seek, or the life you will someday realize you want to live. Without the ongoing support of the powers and blessings you have bottled up inside your mind, it is difficult to make sense of this world and your life. Release the powers of your Life Force and the resourceful knowledge that works in it to help you make sense of your life. A prayer I would suggest for issues that really have you struggling for answers and a little approval, bearing the equation for successful prayer in mind, would go like this:

Life Force + Desire + Faith + Providence = Success

"God's Life Force is within me, it is his way of living through me. God's peace is in my soul, God shines the light of his holy countenance to illuminate my path.

God's guidance is mine now, I and my Father are one. Nobody and nothing can interfere with my life path, because my path is God's path and God's work upon my path can not be delayed. I bring all my endeavors to fulfillment through his holy name. I seek to work in the unique way for which he calls me as an extraordinary child of God. I will prosper in all ways."

How To Bring About Resolution To A Bad Relationship

Relationships are not anymore or any less difficult than any other problem facing you. The principles are still the same, the equation for resolution is still the same, only it requires two people to resolve. That's right, it is possible to fix the situation with one person, if the significant other has an open mind and heart to the resolution of the problems. If it is a good relationship to start and you want to get it back to that plateau, there must be two willing participants to bring about resolution. Therefore there will be two people praying and desiring instead of one.

Does this bring about a faster resolution? It can, if both partners are willing participants and desire a good relationship with each other, the results of the prayer work and the two willing and open hearts and minds could potentially bring about a faster and more concrete resolution. The result of both partners praying and having faith, using the power of their Life Force may be the cohesion necessary in their relationship. But resolution ultimately depends on the partners, their desire, and their resolve.

You do understand that with the power of the Life Force and its amazing powers of healing and reconciliation, that it is possible that one partner praying and desiring steadfastly can bring about resolution. The other partner has to have an open mind so that the strong powers of remedy can affect the non-participating partner. The Life Forces do intermingle, especially in relationships and marriages, so the odds of this working are great, yet not as great as the chance of the relationship working when the two are very desiring participants in all phases of the resolution. The equation for this resolution is:

Life Force + Desire + Faith + Providence = Success

The prayer to pray is as follows:

"I know that God sheds light and power onto the relationship that I have entered into with my partner. I know that God flows through me as Divine Love, Peace, and Harmony. I feel confident and empowered to put back together the relationship that has gone awry, with the help of the God who watches over me and protects me. God has only successful intentions for my life and the lives of my loved ones, so I feel and know that Infinite Wisdom will reveal to me what I need to know to overcome my times of trouble and fear. I thank the Lord for the Life Force that shines within me and assists me to make my life into what I desire it to be."

You Want To Find The Answer?

A man's heart deviseth his way: but the Lord directeth his steps.
Proverbs 16:9

He shall deliver thee in six troubles: yea, in seven there shall no evil touch thee.
Job 5:19

You know the equation is not going to change now. So the equation stays the same with the result being as absolute as any of the other outcomes. The process of using this equation is the exercise of the Life Force that I have written about throughout the book. These exercises bring about resolution and triumph, and they further strengthen the ability to connect to the infinite powers of the Life Force within you.

It is of primary importance to understand that the solution to any question or issue, lies in the question or issue itself. You are to assume that you know the answer to the question, because in fact you do. The answer sometimes remains hidden in the form of mental stumbling blocks that do not permit you to clearly see and define the most appropriate answer.

When stumbling blocks occur, you have to relax. You have to turn the problem or question over to your power of Boundless Knowledge which reigns in your subconscious mind. You have to know that Boundless Knowledge, having all power to answer any question, is locating the answer for you and making it available to you so you can verbalize it or write it down for others to see or execute. Sometimes you need to dig very deep down. The way to do this is to calm yourself, get very relaxed and continue to relax, before too long the answer that fits best will appear to you. It may come to you in a thought or a dream, someone may mention something that triggers the answer, or it may happen in some other way. Rest assured, the answer will come to you.

You must remain unshakably confident the whole while you are seeking the answer to the question or problem with which you are faced. You must feel certain about the outcome. Remember all things that influence your world are born and bred in your world. Your world is everything that your conscious and subconscious minds take in from your surroundings. You can bet they haven't missed the ultimate answer to any question that you see fit to pose to the power of your Boundless Knowledge. The equation:

Life Force + Desire + Faith + Providence = Success

"God's ideas are available in my mind with perfect accuracy. I am perfectly calm and prepared to receive the exquisite answer to the questions I pose today. Please help me to relax into a state of perfect clarity so I can receive the answers that God delivers through the blessing of Boundless Knowledge. I seek this answer as a missing piece to the puzzle that arises at this moment, and I know that God will bless me with resolution in a way that only he can. God works through me and his Divine Power is alive in me, assisting me to peace, joy, prosperity, harmony, wisdom, and love. I feel great peace for the answer comes to me. Thank you Father."

This prayer is so successful. I have been presented with many questions and challenges personally, that I have taken to God in prayer. This prayer, or a variation of it, has been successful for me on innumerable occasions. I have had others that I have suggested to pray a prayer such as this and to their fortune, they did. The outcomes have always been tremendous and without fail. Whenever in a bind, fall onto this prayer and it will stand you up and set you back on the course in a more expeditious manner than before you got sidetracked.

Overcoming The Addictions That Demonize Your Soul

Addictions are a cruel lot in which to make your bed. The troubles that are visited upon those that have obsessive habits of any nature, are paralyzed by them. Dependencies on drugs, alcohol or any other vice that is not socially appropriate or easy to live with, is a hideous burden to carry for any human being. This burden can be lifted with the power of prayer and the knowledge that you do indeed, have the powers within yourself to overcome it.

For I will restoreth health unto thee, and I will heal thee of thy wounds, saith the Lord...
Jeremiah 30:17

Take heart in these words, because the eternal Life Force that lives and works within all people, is able to heal all illnesses that come upon you. All illnesses of the mind, all illnesses of the body, and all illnesses of the spirit can be conquered by the power of the Great Creator and Protector through the power of the Life Force in which he works.
This great gift works in you to help you to overcome the weaknesses of your mind and body that can be directly attributed to the thoughts, ideas, and behaviors that you employ.

You have to come to the realization with your addiction that you are in control and you have the full power of the mind and body to control it day-by-day, week-by-week, and forever. Do not accept the idea that you are powerless to this addiction. Don't let the addiction hold any power over your life, this addiction is an external, and externals have no power except the power that you give to them. The only obstacle to healing an addiction is relinquishing the power that you give to it that makes the addiction strong and your powers weak.

The healing powers or the powers that you give to an addiction are powers that you alone control. Cease giving powers to the addictions that you permit to control your life and take it back for your own pleasure. When you do this, you will see a change in you and you will perceive a change in the people, places, and things around you. Never again will you allow yourself to perceive power or influence in your life, from external factors. Such power simply does not exist, and you weaken yourself in every conceivable way when you believe it does. The equation for success through prayer:

Life Force + Desire + Faith + Providence = Success

You have the Life Force, it resides within you whether you consciously choose to use it at this time or not. If you want to overcome your primary addiction and all tendencies of addiction, you will fuel your desire toward victory over the addiction. The desire will drive your subconscious mind to begin making it happen.

You must have faith. Belief in your own Life Force and its ability to overcome the challenge which is to be destroyed, is of primary importance. You must believe that you have all the powers to be victorious and it will be so. The blessing of providence will work to give you all you need to achieve success in the defeat of your addiction. You can live the rest of your life filled with the glories that God will reward to you for finding and using your true talents and blessings he has bestowed upon you. A prayer to work to this end is as follows:

"I have the great power of the Life Force, which through the power of God, wells up inside of me in order to take down all problems and challenges that I face with a crashing wave of omnipotence. I know my God works in me and through me. I am a temple for his holy works and through him I accomplish all that he knows I desire to accomplish. I feel and know that my mind and body work in perfect harmony together providing me with a solid foundation by which I will ground my faith and love. I look forward to great health and prosperity in the travels to come and I know that the Lord will keep my path straight so that I can marvel in the triumphs of success. I wish love and good will to others and I know that love and good will shall come back to me ten-fold."

Go Out And Make A Difference.

Now take your newfound skills, beliefs, talents, and powers out into the world and show others how the powers given to everyone, stored up in the vast cavern of the subconscious mind, can fix all the wrongs and cure all the ills of the world. Let everyone know that success and happiness is available by fully acknowledging and letting loose all the power of the Life Force to achieve all that you desire.

Go in peace and serve your Lord, for he is great and has given you everything you need to make whatever life you choose for yourself. Thank you!!

Bibliography

Works in this bibliography are not necessarily books that were referred to in the writing of this book, but more importantly they are the books that have helped me shape the foundation of my ideas and thoughts which I have relayed to you in this book. These books have shaped who I am and who I will be. They are the beginning books of a life of learning. They have been the books that I find myself reading and re-reading and it is this constant clarification and finding new meaning in each one of these works that heavily influences the concepts that I have brought forth throughout the pages of this book.

I hope that in time you will make a conscious decision to pick up a few of these books at a bookstore near you. Just as I pray that my book will have a positive and profound impact on your life, I also pray that you will not sell yourself short and limit your new enlightenment to the pages of this one book. I invite you to read these books for pleasure and for improvement of the thoughts and ideals that make you who you are. You are a wonderful human being filled with the promise of those things you wish to accomplish. Go out today and begin to accomplish.

Buckingham, Jamie. Power For Living. 4th edition, 7th printing. U.S.A.: Arthur S. Demoss Foundation, 1999.

Caldwell, Kirbyjon H. The Gospel of Good Success: A Road Map to Spiritual, Emotional, and Financial Wellness. New York: Fireside-Simon and Schuster, 2000.

Frankl, Victor E. Man's Search For Meaning. 1984 ed. New York: Pocketbooks-Simon and Schuster, 1984.

Gibran, Kahlil. A Treasury of Kahlil Gibran: The Arabic Writings By The Author Of The Prophet. Ed Martin L. Wolf. Translated by Anthony Rizcallah Ferris. New Jersey: The Citadel Press, 1974.

Haddock, Frank Channing. Power of Will: A Practical Companion Book for Unfoldment of the Powers of Mind. London: The Pelton Publishing Company, 1915.

Holy Bible. King James Version. U.S.A.: Collins World.

Luther, Martin. Small Catechism. Edited by C. Gausewitz. Milwaukee: Northwestern Publishing House, 1956.

Murphy, Joseph. The Miracle of Mind Dynamics: A New Way To Triumphant Living. New York: Reward Books-Penguin Putnam Inc., 1964.

Reilly, Harold J., and Ruth Hagy Brod. The Edgar Cayce Handbook For Health Through Drugless Therapy. 1975. New York: A Jove Book-Macmillan Publishing Co. Inc., 1982.

Stone, Clement W., Foreword. Success Through A Positive Mental Attitude. 1960. By Napoleon Hill. New York: Pocketbooks-Simon and Schuster, 1987.

Acknowledgments

Special Thanks and Credit
Special thanks, dedication, tribute and memorial to Dr. Joseph Murphy for his God-inspired teachings, preachings, and ideals that were years ahead of their time, yet the truths that he preached had been around forever. His teachings and dedication to the principles of life, and how they are so inspired by God and so much a part of who we are, have driven many men to see beyond their humanity and transcend the challenges and tribulations that keep so many people captive in this earthly realm.

I used a culmination of his ideas and thoughts, which are so wonderfully similar to mine, in part, on pages 9, 11, 12, 13, 14, 17, 18, 19, 23, 25, 26, 27, 30, 38, 39, 43, 47, 51, 52, 53, 56, 57, 58, 59, 60, 61, 72, 77, 79, 83, 91, 97, 99, 101, 103, 104, 109, 113, 120, 123, 125, 126, and 129. I credit the use of some sort of Joseph Murphy thought or ideal on just about every third page of this book. That shows quite impressively what kind of impact his teachings have had on the life that I lead and the thoughts I think. He truly was an amazing man, respected by all and revered by most.

Although I take credit for the thoughts that I think and give praise to God, it is his works that sometimes help me to see the truths of The Creator more clearly and purely. In fact, most of the prayers that I have been praying and I believe others should pray are derived from the simple prayers that he expresses in his writings. There are many variations of prayer and how to pray, but I have always been intrigued by the simple approach that is taken where the gifts prayed for are always given. It is the results we seek that lead us to prayer, and it is only the power and belief in prayer that brings us to which we seek. It is that very truth that makes the Lord so very great, mysterious, and incredible.

A special thanks to Viktor Frankl for such a lovely book telling of the very brutal truths of his life and the lessons that he had learned. To Napoleon Hill for being the leader and founder of books that help people to soar without limits. To Edgar Cayce, who was able to see the future with the gifts of the Lord. He is a man who assisted society in planning for all of the earths changes and every person's individual life-changes.

A wonderful thank you to Frank Channing Haddock for his book which also shares the truths of God with the thoughts of men and comingles them in such a way that to see the gifts of the world as anything less than glorious, is a shame and a shortsighted view. Of course special thanks to a great man, Martin Luther, for breaking down the bible, making it easy to understand and easily categorized by its many facets of truth.

Kahlil Gibran is a true poet, for he speaks the eternal truths of the world as so common place, yet he mixes it with imagery and intensity that it shines like the diamonds of the earth and leaves them sparkling in the mind's eye.

All of these great writer's, poets, teachers, and prophets are an incredible blessing from God. They were each able to turn to their internal powers to re-shape the thoughts, views, morals, opinions, and perceptions of the earthly plane. They take regular men and give them the motivation and impetus to reach beyond this plane and the earthly body, to seek and find the truth that transcends who we are and why we are here.

For each of these truly wonderful and inspired men, I give thanks to God. From age eleven I have known that I have, concealed in the inner-workings of my mind, all of the truths of life and all the solutions to man's challenges and suffering. I will continue to unlock these truths and make known the solutions. I ask that everyone who reads this book do the same for the good of man, in God's name.

www.ingramcontent.com/pod-product-compliance
Ingram Content Group UK Ltd.
Pitfield, Milton Keynes, MK11 3LW, UK
UKHW041846190726
13854UKWH00002B/744